Confessions of a Recovering Racist

CONFESSIONS OF A
RECOVERING
RACIST

George O'Hare *with* Emma Young

NEW YORK

LONDON • NASHVILLE • MELBOURNE • VANCOUVER

Confessions of a Recovering Racist

Published in New York, New York, by Morgan James Publishing. Morgan James is a trademark of Morgan James, LLC. www.MorganJamesPublishing.com

The Morgan James Speakers Group can bring authors to your live event. For more information or to book an event visit The Morgan James Speakers Group at www.TheMorganJamesSpeakersGroup.com.

ISBN 9781683507765 paperback
ISBN 9781683507772 eBook
Library of Congress Control Number: 2017914699

Cover Design by:
Rachel Lopez
www.r2cdesign.com

Interior Design by:
Chris Treccani
www.3dogcreative.net

In an effort to support local communities, raise awareness and funds, Morgan James Publishing donates a percentage of all book sales for the life of each book to Habitat for Humanity Peninsula and Greater Williamsburg.

Get involved today! Visit
www.MorganJamesBuilds.com

To my wonderful wife, Jean O'Hare. Thank you for your patience and understanding and for being the best wife and mother the world has ever known. I love you and I miss you every single day.

TABLE OF CONTENTS

Foreword	*By Father George Clements*	*ix*
Preface		*xiii*
Chapter 1	The Negro in the Desk behind Mine	1
Chapter 2	Racist-in-Training	11
Chapter 3	A Kid Named Podgy	23
Chapter 4	Navy Life	37
Chapter 5	All White College Life	41
Chapter 6	On My Own	47
Chapter 7	Love, Marriage and Sears	55
Chapter 8	The Jaycees & a Hoodlum Priest	63
Chapter 9	Trouble-Making Preacher	69
Chapter 10	Life Changing Friendships	83
Chapter 11	Discovering Soul Music	101
(Photo Album)		*113*
Chapter 12	No More X's	125
Chapter 13	Racism Kills	133

Chapter 14	Soul Train	139
Chapter 15	Stepin Fetchit	143
Chapter 16	Black Man of the Month	149
Chapter 17	Chicago's First Black Mayor	159
Chapter 18	Things White Racists Never Learned	163
Chapter 19	Life after Sears	173
Chapter 20	Association of Recovering Racists	183
Chapter 21	Anti-Semitism	193
Chapter 22	Fake It until You Make It	195
Epilogue		*199*
Acknowledgements		*201*
About the Authors		*203*

FOREWORD

By Father George Clements

People are still being judged and discriminated against because of the color of their skin. Racism is alive and well in America, and it is painful. Racism denies its victims the right to enjoy meaningful employment, the right to live in an area of their choosing, and indeed, the right to live

George O'Hare explains in this insightful, provocative and compelling book that a child does not enter this earth as a racist; we have to be taught to hate. George offers as a testament to this truth, his experience as a child raised in a White, Irish Catholic home, where he mimicked his uncle's racist behavior and employed the "n-word" frequently to win his uncle's approval. He grew up in a racist environment where he learned that taunting and physically abusing Blacks would gain peer acceptance.

Beyond name-calling and abusive behavior, the training George received drilled certain inalienable beliefs into his young, impressionable mind. George and other racists-in-training learned at a very early age that Whites held a superior position over any other race. They learned that Black people were the least intelligent humans in the world, a class of humans (if they were human) to be shunned and feared. From early childhood, through teen years and early adulthood, the lessons of racism had been deeply embedded into George O'Hare's mind, and as a result, by the time he reached his early twenties, George O'Hare was a racist through and through.

Given the depth of these lessons throughout one's formative years, it seemed improbable, if not impossible that one could recover from such a racist upbringing. Becoming a recovering racist is not only possible, as George O'Hare illustrates through his experiences, but it is also necessary if this nation is going to survive. George's strong desire to overcome his racism and the resultant fifty-plus years he spent in various stages of recovery is the thesis of this timely book.

As a person of color growing up in Chicago, the most segregated city in the nation and as a Black priest in a predominately white Roman Catholic Church, to say I am familiar with racism would be an understatement. Racism is nothing new, but what is novel in my estimation is a former white racist dedicating the greater part of his life to its eradication. That is why George's story is so unique.

I was fortunate enough to meet George in the early stages of his recovery from racism. In 1957, I was a young, newly ordained priest at St. Ambrose Church in the Kenwood-Hyde Park area of Chicago. There were only a few Black priests in the entire Chicago Archdiocese, and we would frequently meet to talk about our lack of recognition as fully ordained Roman Catholic Priests. In my second assignment years later at St. Dorothy's rectory, one evening the housekeeper informed me of a visitor in the downstairs parlor. That visitor turned out to be a young white man, a few years my senior, who introduced himself as George O'Hare. "Someone told me there was a Black priest here and I came to see for myself," he said. That curiosity and refreshingly honest candor caused George O'Hare to become one of the most loved individuals that I know. To this day he has not changed. George, and I became friends at that moment and continue to remain best friends.

Over the ensuing fifty-plus years, George developed lasting friendships with some of the most iconic African Americans in the nation. The stories of his encounters with Rev. Dr. Martin Luther King Jr.; Comedian and Activist Dick Gregory; the Greatest Boxer of all time, Muhammad Ali; Honorable Minister

Louis Farrakhan; Reverend Jesse Jackson, Sr.; Jesse Jackson Jr. and many others are engaging, enlightening, inspiring and humorous.

There is much to be done in the battle to rid the world of racism, especially during this era of "Trumpism." The government cannot legislate racism out of existence. It is up to each person to take the first step in confronting his or her racism and beginning the process of recovery. George O'Hare's book helps both racist and victim alike to understand this evil called racism. Let the healing begin.

PREFACE

Confessions of a Recovering Racist is not my life story. It is the story of racism, illustrated by the racist attitudes and behaviors I learned and practiced from my very early childhood into adulthood. It's the story of how the belief that one particular race is superior or inferior to another causes people to act and think irrationally.

As you read through these pages, once in a while you will come across what is now known as "the n-word." That word is not meant to offend; rather it is there to make my story as authentic as possible.

Although no one is born racist, my life became a prime example of how a racist environment and misguided thinking can become instilled into a person's mind and spirit. Lies handed down from one generation of White people to another cause a person to believe White supremacy is a way of life and should always be protected and defended by any means necessary.

This story reflects the tragedy of racism and how it destroys the souls of both the oppressors and the oppressed.

To my fellow White Americans, as you read this book, you can probably relate to some of the experiences I had as a youth; some of the lies taught about "those people"; and the unfounded hostility I developed toward a race of individuals as a result. My desire is that my story will help dispel the lies and free your minds of the hatred, disrespect, and prejudice we learned so well.

To my fellow Black Americans, you too have been lied to about your capabilities, about who you are, and about who your ancestors were. You can help eradicate these lies by teaching your children they come from a race of intelligent, creative, and innovative people. Teach them to hold their heads high and be proud of who they are.

"American exceptionalism with patriarchy, racism and white identity, is literally created from an inhumane, colossal festering wound which whites refuse to acknowledge. So we refuse to begin doing the work to heal it. I think of whites like Alcoholics Anonymous thinks of its members: You are never really not racist as a white person. You may well be a racist in recovery. You may be a functional anti-racist. But you have a sordid history of racism in your past and a propensity for lying to yourself about it. Only constant working towards the destruction of racism—and being an ally to people of color and to indigenous folks—allows you to live another day without being a racist for one more day. Every day is a challenge. But I believe we can rise to this challenge, together."

STEVEN WOLF - *JOURNALIST*

CHAPTER 1

The Negro in the Desk behind Mine

"No one is born hating another person because of the color of his skin, or his background, or his religion. People must learn to hate, and if they can learn to hate, they can be taught to love, for love comes more naturally to the human heart than its opposite."
—NELSON MANDELA

My third-grade teacher at St. Matthews Catholic School was a Dominican nun whose name was Sister Ann Leo. She was tall with dark eyes and dark eyebrows that stood in sharp contrast to her very white face, on which there seemed to be, in my young mind, a very stern frown permanently etched into her features. The previous year, she had been my second-grade teacher; so on the first day of the new school year, I was greatly disappointed to learn she had now become my third-grade teacher. It was just my luck to have the meanest nun at St. Matthews Catholic Elementary School for two years in a row!

In Sister Ann Leo's room, we didn't pick our seats. Each desk had the name of its intended occupant neatly printed in large letters on a big sheet of paper. I began the search for my name at the back of the classroom, hoping to find my desk there, away from the eagle-eyed Sister Ann Leo. No such luck. Once again Sister Ann Leo had put me right up front facing her. With a heavy sigh I took my seat and resigned myself to the fact that this year was going to be like second grade all over again.

Danny Cavanaugh sat at the desk to my left. On the right was a row of empty seats that would never be filled; their sole purpose was to separate the third-grade boys from the third-grade girls. It was like that in every classroom at St. Matthews, and any other Catholic School for that matter. Catholic school administrators seemed to have had a real phobia about girls and boys mixing. In Catholic grammar schools, you would find the young men sitting in one section of the classroom, the young ladies in another, and never the two should meet. Both genders had their designated places in the playground.

It was worse in Catholic high schools. Boys and girls weren't even allowed to share the same school. There were all-girl Catholic high schools, and all-boy Catholic high schools and the few that were co-ed were so strict they may as well have been two separate schools.

I stole a glance at the desk behind mine, pleased to see the name of my friend Arthur Reilly written neatly on a large sheet of paper. Like most of the kids at St. Matthews, Arthur was Irish, yet he and I had a lot more in common than our Irish heritage. We both had drunken uncles.

Arthur's Uncle Pat and my Uncle Lou used to drink together in the same bars. When they got together, they'd complain non-stop about "those damn niggers and Jews."

"Those damn Jews are buying up all the stores and stealing our money with those Jew prices."

"Those damn niggers have got it made with all the free stuff they get, like their food, clothes, and housing in the projects," Arthur's Uncle Pat would say.

Uncle Lou would add, "They don't all live in those housing projects. I know because I rent to some of them, and they damn well better have my rent money on time or I'll put their nigger behinds on the street where they belong."

Then it was Uncle Pat's turn again, "They sit around on their lazy behinds, rolling their eyes, making babies, and making fun of us White people while we work hard and pay taxes."

"So that they can get everything for free!" Uncle Lou interjected.

Arthur and I agreed that those Negroes gave our uncles plenty to complain about. When they weren't complaining about the Negroes, they were telling jokes about them.

After an entire summer without seeing my friend, Arthur, I looked forward to catching up, trading some more Uncle Lou and Uncle Patrick jokes, and passing notes when Sister Ann Leo wasn't looking.

The loud clomping of Sister's shoes interrupted my thoughts. She stopped at the desk behind mine, picked up the paper with Arthur's name on it, crumbled it into a ball, and tossed it into the wastebasket, which was halfway across the room. Sister could throw a crumpled paper ball from anywhere in the room, and it would always land in the wastebasket. On the few occasions when she'd leave the room, we would ball up sheets of paper and try to land them in the wastebasket. By the time Sister would return to a room full of crumpled papers all over the floor, the entire class would be sitting quietly like little innocent angels. Then, as if to say, "This is the way it's done," she would deftly toss the crumpled up sheets of paper, one-by-one, into the wastebasket; like she had just done with the paper with Arthur's name on it.

"Arthur Reilly won't be returning this year," Sister Ann Leo announced. My heart sank.

Children were still coming into the classroom, looking for their names, finding them and taking their seats. Those who hadn't been at St. Matthews the previous year or who had registered late did not have an assigned desk. Sister managed to abandon her stern look long enough to smile at each new student and ask their name as she showed them to their desks.

Suddenly, any pretense of a smile vanished from her face. The class instinctively turned toward the door to see what had disturbed Sister's usual calm, stern countenance. In stunned silence, we looked in the direction of Sister's gaze and immediately understood why she was so shocked, as we sat there, also in shock.

There, about to enter our classroom and shatter our lily-White world stood a little Negro boy. His face was very dark brown and shiny. Uncle Lou once told me that the Negroes put Vaseline on their faces to make them shine like that. His hair looked like the steel wool that Grandma always used to clean her pots and pans. He had the whitest teeth I had ever seen and used them to flash a stupid grin as he stood there, patiently waiting for an invitation into our all-White classroom.

Sister Ann Leo wasn't able to muster up a smile this time, not that she even tried. Never taking her eyes off of the little Negro boy, Sister Ann Leo walked to the empty desk behind mine and pointed to it as she motioned toward him.

"Sit here," she said sternly, never bothering to ask him his name. He took a seat, still wearing that stupid grin that reminded me of Stepin' Fetchit, the happy-go-lucky Negro in the movies.

My father used to take me to see Stepin Fetchit movies at the Tivoli Theater on the South Side of Chicago, which was right next door to his café, known as the Tivoli Tap Room. He even named his big, black Great Dane after Stepin Fetchit. I used to wonder why people called Negroes black when most of them were really brown; some darker brown than others. Once I asked Uncle Lou about that and he said, "Their skin may not be black, but you can bet your bottom dollar their souls are blacker than dirt." This was somewhat confusing because before that he had sworn that Negroes had no souls at all.

As the little boy plopped down in the desk behind mine, he flashed that stupid Stepin Fetchit grin, waiting for me to return the smile. *Well, he can smile all he wants to*, I thought to myself, *but you'll never catch me smiling back at a Negro*. I couldn't have smiled back if I wanted to because I was fiercely holding my breath. Uncle Lou had told me how bad Negroes smelled, and I didn't want to be assaulted by that awful stench.

Of course I could only hold my breath for so long. I had to release it within seconds. When I finally breathed again, to my surprise the little boy didn't smell bad at all. In fact, he smelled all clean and fresh, like the lemony soap Grandma used for my bath. Still, just the thought of sitting so close to a Negro was more than I could bear.

As I surveyed the classroom, looking for an empty desk, I tried to think of an excuse I could give Sister Ann Leo for wanting to move my seat. Saying the sun hurt my eyes wouldn't work because Sister kept the blinds drawn on sunny days so the glare wouldn't prevent us from seeing the blackboard clearly.

My desk was in the very front row, just a few feet from the blackboard, so I couldn't say I was too far away to see. *Should I just tell the truth?* I wondered. *Could I just say, "Sister Ann Leo, may I move my seat because my Uncle Lou doesn't want me sitting too close to niggers?"* Surely she would understand that. She didn't seem to like them very much herself.

The rest of the morning was a blur. Sister Ann Leo wrote something on the Blackboard but I wasn't paying any attention. She must have said something because her lips were moving but I didn't hear a word. That morning, there was only one thing on my little eight-year old mind: the little Negro boy in the desk behind mine.

When the bell rang for recess, we walked out to the playground in a single file. Once we were finally away from the watchful eyes and ears of Sister Ann Leo, all the boys came together and began to see who could say the worst things about the little newcomer.

"Did you see that stupid grin?" one boy asked.

"My father said Negroes don't have any brains, so how can they learn anything in school?" another asked.

"You'd better watch him George, or he'll copy your papers."

On the other side of the playground, the girls were probably doing the same thing.

The new boy was standing by the monkey bars all by himself. Brian Kelly looked his way.

"Hey, Georgie, aren't you going to go play with the new boy?" he teased.

"That's no boy, that's a nigger," I said.

My crude remark made all the kids giggle. I kept it up.

"If we weren't looking I bet he'd take out his tail and swing from those monkey bars."

Little Timmy Boyle was the shortest boy in the class. He was even shorter than me. Now his eyes became enormous.

"He's got a tail?" he said in amazement.

"All Negroes have tails," I said matter-of-factly, "My Uncle Lou told me so."

"How does your uncle know?" Brian Kelly challenged.

"Because he knows everything about them," I said, "He owns all the houses they live in, and I go with him to collect their rent."

That revelation caused all of the children to look at me with a new admiration, as they began to bombard me with questions.

"Do they have furniture in their houses?"

"What do their houses smell like?"

"My mother said Negroes don't have fathers. Did you see any fathers in the house?"

"Do they have food?"

Timmy stole a glance at the new boy whose smile had completely disappeared.

"You think he's waiting for someone to ask him to come and play with us?" Timmy asked.

"Yeah, let's tell him we wanted to play 'Pin the Tail on the Nigger,' but he already has a tail," Brian said. This made everyone laugh.

Timmy and I decided that if he raised his hand to go to the bathroom we'd raise ours too and follow him. Then whatever stall he went into, I would take the stall on one side and Timmy would go into the stall on the other side and we would stand on the toilet seats and peep over to get a glimpse of his tail.

Everyone was laughing hard and looking at the little Negro boy who looked like he was ready to burst into tears. He put his head down and began walking toward the school. I could tell he knew we were talking about him, but I didn't care. He had no business coming to our school.

"Maybe they'll send some more Negroes to St. Matthews so he'll have someone to play with," said Brian Kelly sarcastically. Brian meant that as a mean joke, but not a single one of us thought it was funny. How could he even think that? More Negroes? One was one too many.

Once I had asked Grandma, "How come the Negro kids east of Sacramento Boulevard don't go to St. Matthews?" I didn't say nigger when I was talking to Grandma because she acted like just uttering that word was a sin. "George, that's not nice," she'd say. "It's best to call them Negroes." I figured if saying nigger was wrong, Uncle Lou would have given me a good whipping for it like he did whenever I did anything bad. But whenever I said anything bad about the Negroes or repeated a joke about how dumb or lazy they were, Uncle Lou would just smile and give me that look that made me feel special.

Grandma thought about it a minute before she answered my question. Finally, she said, "Those people are nice, as long as they stay in their place." I wanted to ask where their place is, but Grandma didn't seem like she wanted to keep that conversation going. Anyway, I figured that no matter where their place was, St. Matthews Elementary School wasn't the place for them. *But if it wasn't their place, why did the little Negro boy come there?* I wondered.

Uncle Lou used to tell me, "Negroes are funny when they roll their eyes and do their 'yassuh boss' routine, but that's in the movies. In real life, those people are very dangerous, coming at night to steal your food and rape the women; so it's important to keep the doors locked, always."

At eight years old, I didn't know what the word "rape" meant, but I knew it wasn't anything good, and I knew they only did it to women. I began to ponder it all in my little mind. *If Negroes were only nice when they were in their place, what happens when they are not in their place?* I imagined the little Negro boy coming to our house and stealing our food and raping my Grandma, whatever that meant.

Back in the classroom, I sat facing the front, never daring to look at the little Negro boy behind me. *What if he knew I was talking about him and his "tail?" What if he was angry?* I wondered. When he raised his hand to go to the bathroom, Timmy and I raised ours, too. Sister Ann Leo said only one of us could go at a time, so she let Timmy, go first, then me, and then the little Negro boy who dashed out of the classroom with tears in his eyes. *I should have stayed longer,* I thought, *and then he might have wet himself.* When the school bell finally rang, the class stood up, waiting for the second bell so we could file out of the classroom.

We always walked all the way to the corner in pairs, boys in one line and girls in the other. The nuns were stationed along the way to make sure we didn't talk or get out of line before we got to the corner. To my devastation, I was paired up with the Negro boy. He smiled at me. *Why was he smiling at me after I had*

But Grandma wasn't finished telling the story. "Even the Priest was there," she continued. "The Principal said she understood why we were upset and she doesn't know how it happened."

"But what are they going to do about it?" Uncle Lou demanded.

"She said they'll take care of it, Lou. Now we've just got to trust those nuns and priests."

The next day I went to school, dreading to see the Negro in the desk behind mine. But I soon found out I had nothing to dread. The school day came and ended and to my great relief, he never showed up. From that day until the day I graduated from St. Matthews Catholic School, no other Negro ever set foot in our all-White Catholic school.

CHAPTER 2

Racist-in-Training

"Racism is something you learn, not something you're born with."
—Anonymous

We finally got a new teacher in fourth grade. Sister Frances was a lot different from Sister Ann Leo. For one thing, she didn't wear a perpetual stern frown all the time. Unlike Sister Ann Leo, she didn't pace back and forth with a wooden ruler, ready to strike the knuckles or palms of any child that didn't follow her rules to a "t." In fact, Sister Frances didn't have a long list of rules like Sister Ann Leo. She had a heart of gold and loved everyone. I think that's what got her in trouble.

The nuns used to sell little holy cards to the children. Each card had a picture of a saint on one side and a prayer on the other side. They would charge us a penny for the black and white cards and three cents for the ones they colored with Crayola markers.

One day Sister Frances gave us all a new card.

"Now this is a special card," she said, "We're not going to take this one home; we're going to keep it in our desks, alright?"

"Yes, Sister Frances," we said in unison.

The picture was a Negro man holding a statue of Jesus in one hand and a broom in the other. Uncle Lou told me that Negroes weren't good for anything but sweeping floors. I guessed that even went for the Negroes on the little holy cards.

"This is Blessed Martin DePorres, a Negro. He wasn't a saint, but he was a very good man," Sister explained.

Even though the card was in color, she didn't charge us a single penny for it.

"Now don't forget," she said, "Keep this in your desks and don't take it home."

"Yes, Sister Frances" we obediently said, as we put the cards in our pockets.

When the bell rang, we all filed out of the room, smiling and saying good night to our beloved teacher. Some of the children forgot to put the cards in their pockets and were still holding them in their hands as they were waving goodbye to Sister Frances. That's when she got a strange look on her face.

"Good night, Sister Frances," we said, one-by-one.

She said good night, but that sweet smile had disappeared and was replaced with a look of worry and regret.

We walked in line from school, two-by-two until we got to the corner. Then everyone dispersed and ran home. I couldn't get in the door quickly enough. "Grandma, Grandma, look what Sister gave us!" I shouted, almost out of breath. I thought Grandma was having a small stroke or heart attack when she looked at the holy card with a picture of a Negro on it.

Ordinarily, she would have said, "Now don't let Uncle Lou see this; he'll be furious." But this time, she was too horrified to keep it to herself.

"Lou, come and look at this!"

Boy! Was Uncle Lou mad! He turned a bunch of shades of red. "Where did you get this?" he demanded.

Grandma answered for me. "He got it from Sister Frances at school. I simply can't believe a Catholic nun would do something as awful as give a classroom full of lovely little White children a picture of a Negro. And how dare her say that he's a saint."

"She didn't say he was a saint," I said.

Grandma gave me one of those children-are-to-be-seen-and-not-heard looks.

I didn't think we were getting Sister Frances in trouble by taking the cards home, but as Grandma crossed the room to go to the telephone, I thought about the little Negro boy in my third-grade classroom who was only there one day. Losing Sister Frances would be terrible. She was the nicest nun in the entire school. She would give us candy, even when it wasn't Christmas or somebody's birthday. *Maybe we should have done what she asked and left the cards inside our desks.* I figured it was too late to think about what we should or shouldn't have done.

The next day at school, we had a brand new teacher. Sister Frances didn't leave the school right away. Grandma said she got exactly what she deserved. I don't know what that was. All I know is I never saw her in a classroom again.

If Sister Frances gave us those cards to teach us that Negroes could also be blessed, it didn't work. Maybe she was the one who learned a lesson. Grandma could have told her that Negroes were supposed to stay in their place and that place was not St. Matthews, not even in a picture on a holy card. Any kid who had been in Sister Ann Leo's third-grade class could have warned her not to pass those cards out to a bunch of racist little White fourth graders.

It wasn't our fault that we were becoming racists. Most of my classmates had White, Irish-Catholic parents and like me, they were taught to stay away from "those Negro people." Our parents didn't have anything good to say about Negroes, and neither did any of the nuns or priests at St. Matthews.

The nuns taught us that anyone who did anything beneficial was White, including Jesus Christ, God and Eli Whitney. Eli Whitney was the White man who invented the cotton gin. We never learned about a Negro inventing anything or doing anything worthwhile. The only thing we learned in school about Negroes was that they got lucky and got a free ride from the jungles of Africa to the civilized United States where they were taught to speak English instead of that mumbo jumbo they spoke in Africa. We were taught they should be grateful to be able to live in an apartment or even a house instead of in a hut in the jungles of Africa, surrounded by wild animals. All of the adults seemed to agree that there were only three good people in all of Africa; Tarzan, his wife, Jane and their little boy whose name was Boy.

The movies caused us to believe that all the animals obeyed Tarzan, "King of the Jungle" and all of the Africans worshiped that White man. I thought Tarzan was the best! In one movie, he beat up about a hundred Africans single-handedly. During the summer of 1935, I gained a whole new perspective on Tarzan and a lot of other things.

One of Grandma's favorite questions was, "George, what do you want to be when you grow up?" I never had any real answers until after the summer my Dad enrolled me in St. Bede's Boys Summer Camp in Peru, Illinois. St. Bedes had a swimming pool and instructors. After I learned to swim, I fell in love with the sport. I learned that Johnny Weissmuller, the actor that portrayed Tarzan, was not only "King of the Jungle"; he was a world-famous swimmer, too. I wanted to be just like him. I must have read his book, *Swimming the American Crawl,* at least a thousand times. Johnny Weissmuller, aka Tarzan, was my hero, my role model, and the greatest swimmer in the whole world.

The next time Grandma asked me what I wanted to be when I grew up, I was ready with an answer. "I want to be the world's greatest swimmer," I told her.

Leave it to Uncle Lou to find a racist reason to approve of my decision. "At least you never have to worry about being in the company of a bunch of jigaboos," he said, "They can't swim, and they're scared to death of water."

After thinking about this a little longer, he mused, "Heck, they probably don't even like to bathe."

I thought about my Dad's dog, Stepin Fetchit. "Stepin Fetchit doesn't like to take a bath," I volunteered. Uncle Lou thought that was pretty funny. "Yep, your Dad's good-for-nothing dog is scared of water, just like those good-for-nothing niggers over there east of Sacramento Boulevard."

Racism in the O'Hare home was a family tradition, just like wearing green on St. Patrick's Day, not eating meat on Friday, and going to Mass every Sunday.

Uncle Lou was the most racist one in the family. Racism was so deeply embedded in his mind and spirit, that it defined his entire being. He could not stop hating Negroes any more than he could stop drinking and passing out in bars. When he did pass out, the bartender would call the Chicago Police and tell them that "Husk" O'Hare's brother passed out and they needed them to send some officers to come and get him. The Police Officers would get Uncle Lou from the bar, bring him home, undress him, and put him in bed. Uncle "Husk" would also make sure he compensated the Chicago Police for taking care of his brother.

Everybody knew my Uncle Anderson "Husk" O'Hare who called himself "the Genial Gentleman of the air." He operated as the House Band leader for WGN Radio. At one time, he was the number one orchestra leader in the country and the first to have his band broadcast nationally.

Uncle "Husk" was nowhere near as racist as Uncle Lou, especially when it came to music. He didn't care if the musicians were colored or White, as long as they could play. In fact, he liked the sounds that came from the Negro bands better than the music of the White bands, which he complained was boring and had no rhythm. That kind of thinking got him into a lot of trouble with the super racist musician's union, headed by Jimmy Petrillo. Petrillo eventually kicked Uncle "Husk" out of the union.

Uncle "Husk" introduced me to the sounds of Count Basie and Duke Ellington and, oh, how I started liking their music! I never thought of it as anything but great music, until the night my mother took me bar hopping with her.

When it was my mother's weekend to keep me, she would either take me to one of the beauty shops that she owned and operated, or she'd take me to a bar. Mom was almost as much of an alcoholic as Uncle Lou. Although I never saw her pass out I did see her get drunk plenty of times.

My mother was an extremely good-looking woman, and she had her share of boyfriends. On one particular night, she took me to a neighborhood bar where she met up with one of her suitors. At first, she and the guy were just laughing and dancing and talking. As the evening wore on, they both got pretty drunk, but she was still sober enough to knock his hands away when he started putting them where they didn't belong.

"Not in front of my kid," she would say.

Finally, the guy pulled a handful of nickels out of his pocket and called me to him. "Here kid," he said, pouring the coins into my little hands, "Go play you some music on the jukebox."

I happily headed for the jukebox in the corner of the bar with enough nickels to keep me busy for the rest of the night. Immediately I spied Duke Ellington's name. In went my nickle as I punched the number that corresponded with his song. Then I saw my other favorite, Count Basie. Another nickel and the great sounds of Count Basie echoed throughout the club. I kept this up until someone in the bar loudly called out, "Turn that Goddamn nigger music off!" *What? Was that what I had been playing?* Uncle "Husk" just told me Duke Ellington and Count Basie were two great musicians. He never told me they were Negroes.

I used the rest of my nickels to play some songs by Bing Crosby, the Andrews Sisters, and other White musicians, grateful that this wasn't one of the bars Uncle Lou frequented. What if he had come in and caught me playing that music? I would never have heard the end of it.

The next week, when Uncle "Husk" stopped by the house, he asked me what he always asked, "Did you listen to my broadcast Sunday?" I had my answer ready, and I said it loud enough for Uncle Lou to hear. I knew Uncle Lou would be proud to hear me say, "Yes, you were sure playing a lot of nigger music."

Uncle Lou may have been proud, but Grandma wasn't, "George, I told you it's not nice to say 'nigger'; we call them Negroes," she reminded me.

Uncle "Husk" just shook his head and mumbled something about me being around Lou too much. But Uncle Lou beamed with pride, and that meant the world to me.

My father and Uncle "Husk" were nowhere near as racist as Uncle Lou. When my father wasn't able to take me to the circus or a ballgame and Uncle Lou was too drunk to take on the task, Dad would let Joe Hammer take me. Joe Hammer was the Negro that worked for my Dad, cleaning up his bar and restaurant at night. Maybe if I had spent more time with my father while growing up, my feelings towards Negroes and Mexicans, and Jews would have been different.

But my father was taken away from me too soon, and I was left with my Uncle Lou who instilled in my brain that there were only two kinds of people in the world: those who were White, Irish Catholics and those who wished they were White, Irish Catholics. Many adults would have had enough sense to know that wasn't true, but at eight years old, I had no reason to doubt anything my Uncle Lou said.

Other than naming his big, black Great Dane, Stepin Fetchit, my father didn't have much to say about Negroes one way or the other. The most he would say about them was when we would drive from 63rd and Cottage Grove on the South Side to Grandma's house at 3035 West Washington Boulevard on the West Side. On the way, we would drive past train tracks and when Dad saw the big black steam engines, he never failed to say, "Look at the jigaboos!" To him, the colored were just people to laugh at like the colored actor and comedian, "Stepin Fetchit."

Once I was Christmas shopping with my Dad and we saw two Amos 'n Andy dolls. They had tags on them. One said, "Hello folks, I'se Amos," and the other said, "Howdy folks, I'se Andy." Dad got a big kick out of mocking the way they talked. He got a big kick out of life period; that's why it was so unbelievable that he would die so suddenly and much too soon.

On December 16, 1936, five months before my 10th birthday, my father was shot and killed by a disgruntled patron in his café. His death shattered my world in more ways than one. I never went to St. Bedes Summer Camp again, although I was still in love with swimming. I began going to the YMCA, and my Grandma swore I was committing a mortal sin. "That's the Young Men's *Christian* Association, George," she said, emphasizing the word "Christian" and reminding me that doing anything that was not Catholic was a mortal sin. Christians were certainly not Catholic in her view or in the view of the Catholic Church.

My father's death also meant I never went to the circus or ballgame with his Negro worker, Joe Hammer, again. When my dad was alive, Uncle Lou never said anything about Old Joe Hammer taking me places. But Dad was gone, and Uncle Lou was my guardian. No way was he going to entrust his only nephew to a Negro. I didn't mind not going places with Joe Hammer. To tell the truth, I was a little embarrassed to be with this big, Black Negro, and I was always hoping none of my classmates would see me with him.

Shortly after my Dad's death, my Mom disappeared, and I never saw her again. I had a hard time coming to terms with that. I knew she loved me and we would always have a good time on her weekends. I don't know whether I was more hurt or angry. My father left me but he didn't have a choice. My Mom had a choice and I couldn't figure out why she chose to leave me. With both of my parents gone, the only family I had was my Grandma, Grandpa, Uncle Lou and Uncle "Husk."

Uncle "Husk" was so busy traveling all over America with his bands and doing his radio show on WGN that I only saw him occasionally. On the other hand, Uncle Lou was always there, helping me with my homework, taking me to the ballgames, beating the hell out of me when I did anything wrong, and instilling in me a mistrust, disdain, prejudice and total intolerance for anyone of any other race—especially Negroes.

A few weeks after my father's death, I was helping Uncle Lou put up the Christmas tree, and Grandma was supervising. Somehow we got on the subject of God and whether or not He made mistakes.

"If he doesn't make mistakes," I said, "how come He took my Dad away from me and why did He do it right before Christmas?"

For a minute Grandma seemed like she was at a loss for words. She quickly wiped away a tear, and said, "Maybe God wanted your father to get to heaven in time to enjoy Christmas with Him and the angels."

I knew God had plenty of people with whom he and the angels could enjoy Christmas, and he didn't need my father; but who tries to argue with their Grandma? So, I moved quickly onto what I, in my ten-year old wisdom, had decided was another mistake that God made.

"Why did He make Negroes?" I asked. "Wasn't the world okay when it was just us White people?"

Before Grandma could answer, Uncle Lou started laughing and telling us how what I said reminded him of a joke he had just heard at one of the local bars. Uncle Lou was always telling jokes about Negroes.

"When God was making people and putting them in the oven just long enough to warm their hearts" he said, "Every time a Negro baby would come out of the oven, God would say, 'Oops, I burned another one.'"

I thought that was funny. Even Grandma started laughing. Grandpa came in the room to see what all the laughter was about, so Uncle Lou had to tell the joke all over again, and it was even funnier the second time.

Grandpa just smiled and deadpanned, "If he burned 'em, he should've just thrown them away."

"That's not nice," Grandma said.

"But it's true," Uncle Lou said between chuckles. "Isn't that right, George?"

Still laughing I nodded, yes, it was true. I don't know why that struck me as being so funny: maybe because I knew Uncle Lou wanted it to be funny to me. Uncle Lou tousled my hair grinning.

"That's my boy!" he said proudly.

Chicago has always been a city of neighborhoods. On the West Side where we lived, Sacramento Boulevard was the dividing line between the Whites and the Negroes. There were, of course, further divisions among the White people. There were segregated neighborhoods occupied by the Irish, Polish, Italian, Jewish, or Lithuanians. The different ethnic groups didn't seem to like each other, but when it came to their hatred of Negroes, they forgot their ethnic differences and banded together under the umbrella of "White."

The O'Hare's lived in a third-floor apartment at 3035 West Washington Boulevard. In those days, the water pipes were not hidden behind the walls. Instead, they were exposed, and many times they were used as sort of an intercom system for the building. Two bangs on the pipe meant come to a meeting on the second floor in Mrs. Conroy's apartment. One bang was for Mrs. Hamlin's apartment on the first floor. Grandma didn't use the three bangs for our apartment that often. Once, when I won my first Blue Ribbon for swimming the backstroke, she summoned Mrs. Conroy and Mrs. Hamlin to share in her pride. But during one particular week, the pipes were banging every day; and every day the three women were getting together to discuss the impending invasion of the Negroes from the east. One Negro family had moved west of Sacramento

Boulevard, the possibility of more Negroes coming and eventually taking over the neighborhood terrified the entire community.

We kids did our part to encourage the little Negro kids to stay in their place. Whenever we would see some Negroes on Sacramento Avenue, we'd grab a bunch of bricks and stones and start pummeling them while we chanted "We ha-ate niggers; we ha-ate nig-gers." Now and then, they'd throw rocks back at us, but they mostly ran away as fast as they could. On one occasion, we were throwing bricks at the Negroes, when a brick hit a little Negro in the head. He fell to the ground, holding his head and pretending like he was crying or dying. I probably would have felt sorry for the little Negro boy. However, I knew he was acting. Uncle Lou had already told me that Negroes didn't have any feelings since they were not human.

"What if somebody pulled their tail?" I once asked him.

Uncle Lou thought about it and said, "Yeah, that would probably hurt, I guess that's why they cover their tails up so good."

I figured that little Negro was just upset about seeing all that blood gushing out of his head, *but what did it matter if it was bleeding if it didn't hurt?* I wondered.

I told Uncle Lou the whole story at dinner that night and my take on why I thought the little Negro boy was faking crying.

Grandma said, "George, I don't want to hear about you throwing bricks at anyone. It's not nice."

Uncle Lou said, "I'm proud of you, Son."

Uncle Lou didn't say that very often and calling me son made me feel awfully special. I never did tell him I wasn't the one who threw the brick; even though I have a feeling he still would have been proud of me just for realizing that Negroes fake pain since they can't feel it.

As prejudiced as Uncle Lou was, he was still capitalistic enough to invest in property east of Sacramento and rent the homes and apartments to Negroes. Sometimes I'd ride with him to collect the rent. Usually, they would sit on their porches. I had assumed, as did most of the people in my neighborhood, they had no furniture in their apartments. If they did have furniture, I thought, why would they have to sit out on their porches day and night?

One night I went with Uncle Lou to collect the rent and the tenants were not on the porch, so Uncle Lou knocked on the door. A Negro woman opened the door. Her skin was the lightest of any Negro I had ever seen. When she saw Uncle Lou she gave him the meanest look. Uncle Lou tried to walk past her into her house.

"Good day, Mabel," he said.

She put out her arm to stop him. "Mrs. Martin to you," she said, then added, "You wait right here."

She came back a few minutes later—but she was gone just long enough for me to peep inside. I didn't see much of the tiny little house, but what I managed to see amazed me. She returned with a coin purse and pulled out some bills and handed them to Uncle Lou. Uncle Lou started to count the money.

"It's all there, just give me the damn receipt," she said.

Uncle Lou handed her a receipt and she slammed the door. Uncle Lou was furious.

"Those damn light-skinned niggers think they're good enough to talk to a White man anyway they please," he said. "I don't care how light her skin is, she's still a black nigger to me."

As soon as we got home, I ran in the kitchen where Grandma was fixing dinner. "Grandma," I said, "I went with Uncle Lou to those colored people's houses."

"Don't you always go with him, Little George?" she asked.

"Yeah, but this time was different. We went inside."

Grandma immediately stopped whatever she was doing and shouted. "You went inside?" Now I had her full attention. I nodded yes. Grandma bent down and whispered, even though there was no one around but her and me.

"What did you see?" She quietly asked.

"Tables and chairs and a couch," I said.

Grandma was just as surprised as I had been when I saw the furniture. "They had tables and chairs and a couch?" Grandma repeated in amazement.

My Grandma, like most White people, had no idea what was on the inside of a Negro's house, so she just made up in her mind that their houses were empty.

I guess she thought they just sat on the floor, or their seats were orange crates, or they lived outside on their front porches.

Someone once said prejudice is a result of ignorance; a type of ignorance which fuels racism. Adults told us children all sorts of myths about Negroes; not only that they had no furniture, but they were afraid of water, they had no brains, they had tails, and the list goes on. We believed it all, no matter how ridiculous it sounded. We were racists-in-training, internalizing the same disrespect and hatred our family members had for "those people."

CHAPTER 3

A Kid Named Podgy

"One of the worst things about racism is what it does to young people."
–**ALVIN AILEY**

My father had planned for me to go to Bishop Quarter's Junior Military Academy after I graduated from St. Matthews's grammar school. It was a great, all-White Catholic boarding school for boys. After I had graduated from there, I was supposed to go to Notre Dame University. Dad had plenty of money and could have afforded all of that with no problem, but those plans went up in smoke after he was shot and killed.

Grandma and Grandpa were on fixed incomes. Uncle Lou was a marketing genius and a great salesman who could have made decent money on his commissions. The only problem was he couldn't earn a commission when he wasn't working, and he wasn't working when he was drunk, which was most of the time. So between Grandma, Grandpa and Uncle Lou, there wasn't enough money to keep me in Catholic school.

My famous Uncle "Husk" O'Hare, as well-known as he was, didn't have very much money. That's because after Jimmy Petrillo kicked him out of the union, it was hard for him to get bookings.

The public school that served the district in which we lived was Marshall High School Attending Marshall High School was out of the question for me, because it had a large population of Jewish students. Plus, Negroes were rapidly moving into the area and into the classrooms of Marshall High.

"I am not going to have Little George going to school with a bunch of niggers and Jews," Uncle Lou declared.

He was even willing to move out of that district to protect me from having to attend school with Negroes and Jews. Fortunately, we didn't have to move because he had a friend who lived in the Austin High School District. Uncle Lou enrolled me in Austin High from his friend's address, and gave me a piece of paper with the address on it. "Now keep this in your pocket at all times," Uncle Lou would say, "and if anyone asks you where you live, you tell them, 219 North Leamington; if you forget and tell them your real address, they'll send you to the school with the Jews and niggers."

Since we didn't live in the Austin district, I had to get up early. It took me longer to get to school, but it was worth it. Austin High was a beautiful school. Both of my uncles, Lou and "Husk," and my father, George Sr., had gone there. In fact, that's how Uncle "Husk" got into music. He used to head up the high school orchestra. That band is now in Jazz history books, referred to as the Austin High School Gang. They were famous for playing jazz music at parties. After he graduated, he continued to promote bands.

Austin High wasn't *mostly* White; at that time it was *all* White—White faculty, White administrators, White students, even the janitors were White. "And it had better stay that way," stated Uncle Lou. His greatest fear was Jews and Negroes moving into the district and the school, being public and financed by tax dollars, would not be able to turn those people away. I wasn't concerned. Uncle Lou had drummed it into my head about how dumb Negroes were. "Don't worry, Uncle Lou," I told him, "High School is much harder than grammar school and as stupid as the Negroes are, they would have a hard time skinning and grinning their way through Austin High." I loved to see the look of pride in

Uncle Lou's eyes when I talked like that. I don't know what fueled my racism the most—the hatred toward Negroes that Uncle Lou had drummed into my little head; or my desperate need for his approval.

My life changed dramatically during my first year of high school. First, Uncle Lou heard on the radio one night that the Japanese had bombed Pearl Harbor, so he immediately enlisted in the Navy. It was just Grandma and Grandpa and me living in our little flat. Uncle Lou was stationed at the Great Lakes Naval Base. Whenever he got a chance to get away from the Base, he'd come and see about us. He was especially worried about Grandma because she wasn't getting around like she used to. One day I came home from school to see the ambulance taking my Grandma. She never did come home. Grandpa was never the same after that. He would just sit around and look into space. Uncle Lou said he was going to have to put Grandpa in a nursing home, but Grandpa died before that happened. Losing my Grandma was the saddest thing I had ever experienced next to losing my Dad and Mom. Uncle Lou rented an apartment for both of us, but I was there mostly by myself. By my third year of high school, Uncle Lou rented a room for me at the Local Austin YMCA on Central Avenue on the West Side.

Austin High School had a great campus, with two huge buildings and each one had a swimming pool. Getting on the swimming team wasn't difficult at all. It was the football team that most of the kids wanted to join. Austin's football team was known to be the best high school football team in the nation. Such recognition was due to the hard work of Austin's football coach, Bill Heiland. Coach Heiland would go to schools all over the city to recruit the best players to transfer to Austin High.

When Mr. Heiland went to Dunbar Vocational School to scout out a particular player, the news got around quickly. That's because Dunbar was an all-Negro high school on the South Side of Chicago. No one could figure out why he would go to an all-Negro school to get a good football player. That was the topic of discussion for weeks.

"The guy he's looking at has got to be White."

"Yeah, whoever heard of a Negro being outstanding in football?"

"Whoever heard of a Negro being outstanding in anything?"

"But why would a White kid go to Dunbar Vocational High School?"

"And his name is Podgy, Podgy Simmons. What kind of name is that for a White kid?"

"What kind of name is that for any kid?"

As it turned out, Podgy Simmons was a Negro.

"I'm glad I'm on the swimming team and not the football team," I quipped. Actually, I was glad that Uncle Lou didn't come to the football games, because I'm certain that if he had known there was a Negro at Austin High, he would have taken me out of the school.

"I'm glad he's offense and not defense," someone else said. "Who would want to get tackled by a nigger?"

"Who would want to do anything with a nigger?" I said, but quickly shut up as I saw Mr. Heiland coming down the hall with Podgy Simmons.

Seeing Podgy up close reminded me of the kid that sat behind me for a day in the third grade. Podgy had that same kind of grin. *What could these Negroes be so happy about?* I wondered.

"Which one of you is George O'Hare?" Coach Heiland asked.

I raised my hand, but I was wondering what the football coach would want with a member of the swimming team. I didn't have to wonder long.

"Heard you don't have a locker mate," Coach Heiland said.

A sense of dread came over me as I slowly nodded my head to confirm what he had heard.

"Well, congratulations!" the Coach said, "You have the honor of sharing a locker with the star football player of Austin High, Podgy Simmons."

If that was supposed to make me feel better about sharing my locker with a Negro, it sure didn't work. I wondered if he was as dumb as Uncle Lou said all Negroes were. *White kids have to work hard and pass all kinds of tests to get into high school,* I thought, *but here's a Negro who probably can't read or write, and he gets into an all-White high school just because he's good at playing football.*

Podgy and I never became friends, and although I hated the fact that I had to share a locker with him, I also respected him for what he did for our football team. There's a strange phenomenon that happens even among the most racist White people when a Black person excels in a sport or entertainment. Their performance seems to put a pause on racism, at least where they are concerned.

Nobody could tackle or outrun Podgy. He was a great player in every way. And if somebody said, "Look at that nigger run," someone else would say, "That's no nigger, that's Podgy Simmons."

Thanks to Podgy, Austin High maintained its championship status during the entire four years he attended the school. As for Negroes being dumber than a box of rocks, well, I had taken that for the truth. However, when I thought about it, Podgy Simmons had a whole lot of books, and he must have been doing something with them. So while they might not have been dumber than a box of rocks, I figured, they sure were dumber than White people, even Pollack's, who Uncle Lou said were the dumbest people God ever made.

There was one Polish kid in my Division who was always telling jokes about how stupid Poles were. A Polish man walks up to the store clerk and says, "I'd like a Polish Sausage." And the guy says, "You must be Polish." The man says, "Why, because I asked for a Polish Sausage?" "No," says the clerk, "because this is a Hardware Store." That kid enjoyed his jokes better than we did. But Negroes were the brunt of most of our jokes. We'd go through the halls of Austin High, chanting: "Watermelon, barbecue, Cadillac car; we're not as dumb as you think we is."

Uncle Lou told me a lot of things about Negroes that turned out not to be true. The worst lie he told me was that Negroes had tails. He told me that from the time I was a little kid, but I didn't learn how untrue it was until I was entirely grown. All the while I was in high school, every time Podgy would walk away from the locker I'd just stare after him, trying to envision his tail, and wondering how he hid it so well.

My two best friends at Austin High School were Roland Ludivico Orsucci and Don Emerson. Up until then, I continued to believe that there were only two kinds of people in the world, those that were Irish-Catholic and those that wished they were Irish-Catholic. Ironically, neither Roland nor Don was Irish. Roland whose nickname was "Moose" was Italian and Don was Swedish.

In those days, White people only wanted to associate with other White people, not Negroes, nor "Spics" (what we called the Spanish people), nor "Pollack's" (that's what we called the Polish people). We called Italian people, "Dagos," but Roland was an exception—he was my friend. I had to forgive him in my heart for being a Dago, because of all the ethnic groups that Uncle Lou hated, including "Pollacks," "Chinks" (Chinese), "Spics" and "Dagos," he hated the "Dagos" the most. When I got older and learned about how Hannibal went through Italy raping all of the women, I understood what Uncle Lou meant about Italians being a step up from Negroes. Technically, since Hannibal was an African, I figured Italians must have as much African blood in them as Negroes did.

Even though Don wasn't Irish or Catholic, what we had in common was more important to me—we both loved to swim, and we were both backstroke swimmers.

After my sixteenth birthday, every summer found me on lifeguard duty either at the all-White Oak Street Beach or the all-White North Avenue Beach. It's been said that the swimming pool is one of America's most racist institutions. If you visited either of those two beaches back then, you'd find that truer words have never been spoken.

Most of my lifeguard duty consisted of swimming. I spent a very small percentage of the time sitting up in the lifeguard chair, looking for either a potentially drowning individual, or someone who had violated one of the many rules of the Oak Street or North Avenue Beach. Once when I was backstroke swimming on the beach, I heard a lot of commotion. I looked to see two Negro boys, about fifteen or sixteen years of age. Somehow they had mustered up the audacity to come to our all-White beach. I joined the other White lifeguards yelling at them, "Go on, Nigger!" "Get out of here!" As the group of us approached them, they turned around and ran. If that had been one of the days when I was at the beach alone, I wouldn't have had the courage to yell at them like that or chase them off.

On another occasion, three or four Negroes came to the Oak Street Beach. This time, as we began pursuing them, there were enough of us to approach them from all sides. The only direction in which they could run was toward the water, but they only got so close. Then the look of panic and fear came over nearly every one of those Black faces. That look told us everything—they were afraid of water and probably couldn't swim. We began stampeding them, throwing them in the water. "Drown them, drown them!" we howled. I can't explain the adrenaline rush I experienced.

Trying to drown the Black kids wasn't just about protecting our beach; it was about preserving our race. *What if these people took over our beach? Where would we swim? Next, they would take over our cities, and we'd have nowhere to go.*

I was a little guy, so I found the smallest one in the bunch and gave him a good shove. Splash! He was in the water with the others furiously thrashing for their lives, with no lifeguard to rescue them. After all, it was the lifeguards that were throwing them into the water.

No one drowned that day. Somehow they managed to get out of the water and run for their lives. I suspect there may have been a few White lifeguards who were humane enough to help those poor souls. Or maybe they just didn't want to have to answer to the law about a drowning. It wasn't that the White police patrolling our beaches cared about Negroes drowning, but there were probably some bleeding heart White folks that would have raised hell about it and closed down our beach.

Negroes weren't the only ones that drew the wrath of the all-White lifeguards at the all-White North Avenue and Oak Street beaches. We didn't like the Mexicans or Spics as we called them, and we made them aware of it in much the same way we let colored people know they were not welcome.

As much as we hated Negroes and Jews and Mexicans, we hated homosexuals even more. We had all kinds of names for them, "homos," "faggots," "queers" and we would call them every one of those names. Why we hated them so, I don't know. Maybe it was because we sincerely believed the greatest kind of person God made was the White male. We just couldn't understand why someone who was privileged enough to have been born a male would want to be a female. That baffled me to no end.

Some of the "faggots" tried to come on the beach a couple of times. Each time, instead of chasing them away, we immediately tried to drown them. They were pretty strong, and once when I shoved one, he shoved me back. That scared me because I had heard how mean the sissies could be. After that, I would just stand back and yell, "Drown the "faggots!" "Drown the "faggots!" As far as I know, we never drowned any homosexuals either.

There was one "sissy" named Jimmy Hall, who would come to the beach almost every day, and for some reason, we didn't bother him. That could have been because he didn't hang out with a group—he was always by himself; or maybe because he was so gay, messing with him would be the same as bullying a girl. He was as close to being a real girl as any homosexual I had ever seen.

One day I was sitting on the beach alone when this middle-aged White woman came up to me. Her eyes were darting back and forth, surveying the beach as if she was looking for something or someone.

"Excuse me, Lifeguard," she said as she approached me, "I'm looking for Jimmy Hall." My first thought was, why would this nice woman be looking for that "faggot"? "Have you seen him?" she asked.

"No Ma'am, I haven't seen her I mean him today," I said, expecting her to laugh at my attempt at humor, but she didn't seem to catch the joke. Didn't she know he was a "fag"?

"That's my son. If you see him, please let him know his mother is looking for him," she said as she strode off.

I watched her leave, feeling a little guilty about making fun of him, even though she must have known what he was. *His mother?* I said to myself. Somehow, I never thought of gays having mothers, but here, Jimmy Hall had a mother who would come all the way to the beach to look for him. That incident taught me that gays are real people. Yet, it didn't stop me from hating them, or from hating the Negroes, the spics, the wetbacks, the Pollacks, the Jews, the Lithuanians and the Dagos—except for my friend, Roland Ludovico Orsucci—who was my best friend. Roland (who changed his name to Ron Orr) died while I was writing this book. I will miss my friend very much.

The fact that Jimmy Hall had a mother or that Podgy Simmons could run with a ball did not diminish the racism or homophobia that I had learned throughout my childhood or my teen years or as a young adult. Yes, Podgy Simmons had a locker full of books and he excelled in football, but he was an exception. I convinced myself that he wasn't like the other 99.9 percent of Negroes who we learned were inferior, lazy, shiftless, and dangerous. One or two exceptions didn't matter. We learned that White people were the kings, supreme—White supremacists—and we knew we were right because we were White, and White was always right.

Besides being a lifeguard during the summer months, I would also compete in the swimming meets throughout Illinois that were hosted by the State of Illinois Swimming Association. Every time I heard or read there was going to be a swim meet, I would call and request an application. I went to all of them.

Hinsdale South High School in Hinsdale, Illinois, was near my home and it had a pool. I told the Hinsdale South High School coach that I was participating in swim meets and asked if I could practice in his pool. He had no problem with that and gave me a schedule of times when the school would not be using the pool. I'd go and practice 50-yard sprints, rest a few minutes, do 50 yards fast, and then start all over again: sprint, rest, swim fast. I'd spend hours practicing until I perfected my backstroke.

After this training routine, I'd go to a swim meet and always come away with a Blue Ribbon or Gold, Silver, or Bronze Medal. I usually took first place, but even if I didn't, I would always win some kind of award. Once, I came in fourth place in the Annual Chicago Four Mile Lake Michigan Marathon. Nonetheless, the *Chicago Herald American* reporter, passed up the first, second, and third place winners just to interview me. He couldn't understand how I managed to come in fourth place out of two hundred free-stylers when I was swimming a backstroke.

To attract a big audience and newspaper sports reporters to the meets, the State of Illinois Association would invite a celebrity swimmer to present the awards. The person that drew the largest crowds was Adolph Keifer, known as one of the most famous competitive swimmers in the world. He had set the world record for backstroking—swimming the 100-meter backstroke in 57.9 seconds—and he had won the gold medal in the men's 100-meter backstroke in the Summer Olympics in Berlin, Germany. I won plenty of awards, and it wasn't long before Adolph Keifer knew me by name and acknowledged me each time he presented me with a blue ribbon, plaque, or medal.

I graduated from Austin High School in June 1948. Uncle Lou, Uncle "Husk," and Aunt Vivian came to my graduation. I didn't have to worry about Uncle Lou being drunk and embarrassing me since he never took another drink after enlisting in the Navy.

After Uncle Lou was discharged from the Navy, he rented an apartment for him and me. I was extremely happy to be out of the YMCA. Although it was a great place to be in terms of swimming, it had too many restrictions. I couldn't even have company in my room at the Y. Visitors would have to come to the lobby and I'd come downstairs. Not that I had a lot of visitors. I was pretty introverted.

With Navy days behind him, Uncle Lou began pursuing the love of his life once again: sales and marketing. He never spoke of himself as an ex-alcoholic; he always said he was a "recovering" alcoholic. One thing he hadn't recovered from and wasn't planning to ever recover from was his racism.

Back then, people seldom used the word "racism." The more acceptable term was "prejudice." I would say every White person was prejudiced toward Negroes, but not all of them hated Negroes like Uncle Lou and I did. My Uncle "Husk" and his wife Aunt Vivian viewed Negroes as human beings, even though they never considered them to be equal to Whites. They thought of them as people they might hire to work as doormen, shoeshine boys, or musicians, but not someone who should be in an office position or any professional job. And they certainly wouldn't socialize with them. I didn't share Uncle "Husk's" liberal views. After all, Uncle Lou raised me, and taught me everything I knew; including how and why I should hate Negroes.

Uncle Lou took great pride in his disdain for Negroes, in spite of the fact that it was a Negro doctor who cured him of the rash he had gotten while he was in the Navy. That rash was super ugly and horribly painful; to make matters worse, it itched like crazy. Uncle Lou went everywhere looking for a doctor that could cure it. If somebody told him there was a cure on Mars, he would have been the first man in outer space; he was just that desperate to get some relief from his rash.

Uncle Lou took everyone's advice and tried every salve, pill, and remedy anyone suggested. Nothing worked. He went to all of the doctors that were recommended to him, yet the rash kept getting uglier and more painful.

One day a friend of his told him he heard there was a pretty good dermatologist on the South Side of Chicago. Now, that was like saying there was a cure in the middle of a Negro war zone. Uncle Lou purposely avoided the South Side of

Chicago because that's where all the Negroes lived. When he heard about this doctor he automatically assumed he was White. After all, Uncle Lou taught me and firmly believed Negroes had no brains. And without brains, how could any one of them ever be a doctor?

It never occurred to him that a Black person could be smart enough to become a doctor, especially one who specialized in diseases of the skin. He figured if they knew so much about skin, they would know how to make their skin white.

He determined this doctor was not only White and intelligent, but also brave—brave enough to set up a medical practice in the middle of a Negro community. Furthermore, Uncle Lou decided if this doctor was brave enough to be on the South Side of Chicago, then he would just have to muster up the courage to go there to see him.

"What's the doctor's name?" he inquired of his friend.

"Dr. T.K. Lawless," his friend answered, "By the way, he's a Negro doctor."

This revelation hit Uncle Lou like a ton of bricks. He was about to say, "Forget it," but the rash sent a pain searing through his body. All he could say was, "What's the phone number and address of this Negro doctor?"

When Uncle Lou's friends asked him about the physician he was going to see, he just said "a new doctor." He wouldn't dare tell them he was going to see Dr. T. K. Lawless, because immediately they'd say, in astonishment, "The Nigger doctor?" Uncle Lou was proud of his reputation as a super racist and knew he'd never be able to live down the fact that he was desperate enough to go to a Negro physician.

Uncle Lou made his way to the South Side of Chicago. Dr. T. K. Lawless had an office inside of his home, which was a beautiful mansion on 43rd and South Parkway Avenue (South Parkway Avenue later became Dr. Martin Luther King Drive). The large waiting room barely accommodated the many, patients waiting to hear their name called. Uncle Lou had to live through the ultimate humiliation of having to wait until Dr. Lawless called in all the patients who had come before him, some of whom were White, but many, far too many, were Black. He knew that it was only right for the White patients to be called before him since they were calling names on a first come-first served basis. However, he just couldn't reconcile having a Negro called before his name was called, no matter what time the Negro may have arrived.

Deep down in his racist heart, he knew that Dr. T. K. Lawless wouldn't be able to help his rash. How could a Negro doctor possibly be any better than or even as good as the White doctors he had already seen?

Finally, Uncle Lou was called into the examining room. Dr. Lawless examined the rash and then began to ask Uncle Lou some questions.

"What do you eat?"

"Everything,"

"What do you like to drink?"

"Well, I used to booze it up pretty good, but I don't drink alcohol anymore. I drink soda pop instead.

"How much soda pop do you drink?"

"A whole lot."

"Do you drink water?"

"A little bit."

Dr. Lawless explained that a little bit of water was not enough; and if Uncle Lou wanted to get rid of the rash, giving up soda pop would be his only option. He also told him he would have to start drinking bottled spring water, lots of spring water to help flush out the toxins and acid caused by all of the soda pop he had been drinking.

Giving up soda pop was a hard thing for Uncle Lou to do, but the rash was painful and ugly enough to make him try anything. He bought cases and cases of bottled water, and he drank bottle after bottle after bottle. Drinking the water and giving up the pop worked. His rash went away completely. That's when he stopped saying "that Negro doctor" and started telling his friends "Dr. T. K. Lawless is the finest dermatologist in the USA." This experience by no means cured Uncle Lou's racism. As far as he was concerned, Negroes were still no good: they were lazy and had no brains; but Dr. T. K. Lawless, in Uncle Lou's opinion, was like Podgy Simmons, a rare exception.

As I sat in the auditorium at my graduation, I kept looking back at Uncle Lou, Uncle "Husk," and Aunt Vivian. They were all beaming with pride, waiting for me to go up and receive my diploma. I knew I was going to get an award for outstanding performance as a member of the Austin High School swimming team, which would make them even prouder.

Of course, Podgy Simmons would get a lot of awards for helping Austin's football team get through four years undefeated. I never told Uncle Lou that a Negro was attending Austin High or that I was sharing a locker with him. Well, he was going to find out soon enough that Austin High wasn't as lily-White as he thought, but it was too late to take me out of Austin—I was already out. I had graduated.

All of the graduates sat with their school division room. Since my division came before Podgy's, I had received my diploma and was back in my seat before they called his name. When Podgy walked across the stage, I turned to sneak a look at Uncle Lou. His face had turned beet red. I knew I was going to get an ear full when we left there. I received a couple of medals for swimming, just as I expected. What I hadn't expected was to see Podgy going up on the stage so many times. He got awarded the Most Valuable Player and some other awards from the football team, but then to my dismay, he received even more awards for his academic performance. He got scholarship offers from a dozen schools. I knew I would never hear the end of that. And I was right.

We went out to dinner afterward. Uncle "Husk" and Aunt Vivian gave me a Savings Bond and Uncle Lou gave me a watch. Uncle Lou didn't have very much to say throughout the evening, but when we got home, after Uncle "Husk" and Aunt Vivian said their goodbyes, Uncle Lou let me have it.

"Who have I told you are the dumbest people in the world?"

"Negroes."

"Dumber than dogs, right?"

"Right."

"Then how does it happen that my only nephew didn't get as many academic awards as the Negro did?"

I started to say I guess he's smarter than me, but the words stuck in my throat. No way was I ever going to admit to being dumber than a person who belonged to the dumbest race on earth.

"The teachers had to give him good grades so he could stay on the football team."

Uncle Lou liked that answer. "So in other words, the teachers cheated?"

I nodded. Of course, that was the only valid explanation. Podgy didn't even look smart to me. Uncle Lou didn't seem upset anymore. But just to make sure, I added one more commentary.

"The only thing Podgy Simmons probably knew how to do was run with a ball, and even a dog could do that," I said.

That pleased Uncle Lou to no end. "That's my boy," he said, tousling my hair as he always did when I did or said something to make him proud.

Uncle Lou never mentioned Podgy again. The only thing he said about the graduation ceremony was, "Little George was the smartest kid in the class and the best swimmer."

High school was over. I had completed that chapter in my life, and now it was time to figure out what I would do next. I hadn't given too much thought to what I would do with my life, except swim.

CHAPTER 4

Navy Life

"The United States has the largest and best Navy in the world."
—ROBERT ZUBRIM

Roland "Moose" Ludivico Orsucci, Don Emerson and I remained best friends throughout our high school years. The three of us knew that after high school, the inevitable thing to do was to enroll in college and pursue a degree. We also were aware of how expensive it would be to attend college.

"Do you know about the GI Bill?" I asked Moose one day.

"Yeah, they pay for college, but for only two years. Plus, we're not GIs," he reminded me.

"We could be," I said.

Even though the war had ended a couple of years earlier, the draft still remained.

"If we wait for the government to select us, we'll end up in the Army with a bunch of crazy Negroes," I volunteered.

"Who told you that?" "Moose" asked.

Before I could answer him, he and Don said "Uncle Lou" in unison as if they had rehearsed it. Then they both laughed. They were right. Uncle Lou also told me my best bet would be to follow his and Uncle "Husk's" footsteps and join the Navy.

"Moose" liked the idea of the Navy. He loved football, and the Navy had a pretty good football team. "I know what part of the Navy you love," "Moose" said. Without him telling me, I already knew he was right. The Navy had swimming pools all over the country, and I knew that somehow I would be swimming in most, if not all of them.

Don didn't sign up with "Moose" and me, but he did join the Navy. And as fate would have it, all three of us ended up stationed together at the Great Lakes Naval Station.

On the bus ride to Great Lakes Boot Camp, I began to wonder if getting on the Navy's swim team would be as easy as I had hoped. All the negatives started to pop into my head. *What if they had enough sailors on the swim team and didn't need any more? What if others were signing up that could swim better than me? What if they assigned me to some other duty that conflicted with the swim meets? What if I went through the entire two years in the Navy and never got to swim?* Still mulling the "what if's" in my mind as I got off the bus and so engrossed with my negative thinking, I was startled when I heard a voice say,

"George O'Hare!" "What are you doing here?"

I turned and found myself looking squarely into the face of the great backstroke swimmer, Adolph Keifer. I was surprised that he remembered me, and I told him so. "How could I forget, with all of the awards I presented to you?" he said. He asked me where I was going and I told him it was my first day, and we were headed to boot camp.

"Do you want to be on the swimming team?" He asked.

Did I? More than anything in the world. "Yes, I do," I answered.

"Okay, give me your serial number," he said. Keifer was the Officer in Charge of Swimming for the whole United States Navy! Now that was one "what if" I hadn't thought of.

Next thing I knew, I got a call from the commanding officer.

"I hear Adolph Keifer is a friend of yours," he said.

"Yes, sir."

"Well," he said, "he wants you on the swimming team."

Swimming defined my life in the Navy. I never marched, I never had to attend any presentations, and I barely wore Navy Whites or Navy blues—just my blue and white swim trunks.

One day, one of the captains called me into his office. "George, we need someone to teach swimming, and I'm confident that you can do it," he said. He was more confident than I was. As soon as I got a break, I went to the bookstore and bought a book by the Red Cross on how to teach swimming.

I taught two classes. One was all White; the other all-Negro. Having a class full of Negroes helped dispel the myth that Negroes didn't swim because they were afraid of the water. The truth of the matter was most of the Negroes were from the South where they weren't allowed to go near the White man's pool, and there weren't any pools for Negroes. They told me that sometimes, some of them would swim in the lagoon or creek or in the part of the beach that was sectioned off specifically for Negroes, which was the most dangerous part of the water.

Teaching Negroes to swim wasn't an easy task—especially the "hands on" part of the experience. Luckily, I didn't have to do too much touching. When a Negro under my tutelage became a proficient swimmer, it was quite an accomplishment. Thank God for the Red Cross Book *How to Teach Swimming*. It was like teaching a dog a new trick.

Outside of swimming, I didn't have much to say to the Negroes. Most of them were Mess Men. The U.S. Navy never had a Negro warrant officer or commissioned officer during my entire enlistment. During that time, we used to hear a lot about a sailor named Dorie Miller. Dorie Miller achieved his status as a legendary hero by saving his crew during the Pearl Harbor attack. I just naturally assumed that Dorie Miller was a White person, because I knew White people would never praise a Negro the way they praised Dorie Miller. When I found out, years later, that Dorie was a Negro, I was totally shocked. Dorie Miller was a Mess Man Third Class and even though he received a medal for bravery for getting hold of one of the guns and shooting at the enemy, the Navy never promoted him beyond the rank of Mess Man.

Life in the Navy mirrored civilian life, especially when it came to race relations. Negroes still had to stay in their place, which was cleaning up after the White sailors finished eating, shining officers' shoes, and cooking and serving the White sailors and those with rank. When they went into town, their Navy uniforms didn't mean anything; they encountered the same kind of racism which was prevalent throughout the U.S. People still called them by the "n-word," and they weren't allowed to drink out of the same fountains from which White people drank. Restaurants welcomed sailors, but not the Negro sailors. They had to enter in the restaurants through the back door and take their food out. I didn't feel sorry for them. I just knew that was the way it was and that was the way it was supposed to be. I believed with all my heart that God made the White man supreme.

After serving two years in the United States Navy, it was time to go back home and do something with my life. The G.I. Bill only paid for two years of college, so Moose and I decided to go to Wright Junior College for the first two years since Junior Colleges were almost free. We agreed that after we completed junior college, we would use the G.I. Bill for the last two years of a four-year college. By this time, "Moose" had changed his name from Roland Orsucci to Ron Orr.

CHAPTER 5

All White College Life

"There is a time and place for everything and it's called college."
—BILL COSBY

At Wilson Junior College, White students probably outnumbered Blacks at least three or four to one, possibly more. Still after two all-White schools, and Navy life where the few Black sailors were very subordinate and stayed in their place, it was somewhat of a culture shock to see so many Negroes sitting in the classrooms and walking the halls as if they belonged there. The races segregated themselves from each other. There was no such thing as a Negro sitting next to a White person if it could be helped, and in most cases it could. We didn't make friends with them, and they didn't seem to be anxious to make friends with us. Most of the professors were White, and they seemed to be just as wary of the Negroes as the White students were. There were no warm-fuzzy teacher-student relationships between the White professors and the Negro students. As a result, the "Stepin Fetchit" grin was absent from the faces of the

Negroes attending Wilson Junior College most of the time. They walked the halls, sat in the classroom, always with a sober, somewhat sad look on their faces. They probably dreaded being there as much as we dreaded seeing those Black faces every day.

One April day, Moose, Don and I were walking through the campus when we heard a commotion. We turned to see where it was coming from, and all we could do was stare. A group of Negro students were exuberantly shaking each other's hands, cheering and laughing, with the biggest smiles on their faces. Ordinarily they would have stopped when a group of White students walked past; but they didn't seem to see us and if they did, they didn't care.

The three of us hurried past them, not daring to look, but wondering what in the world could have happened to make those Negroes so happy. As we turned the corner we saw another group of Negroes who were just as joyous as the ones we had just walked past. We were beyond curious, but we agreed that we'd just have to keep wondering because there was no way we were going to ask the Negroes, "What are you boys and girls so happy about?" Instead we just joked about it.

"I don't know what they could be so happy about," I said, "Ol' turncoat Abe Lincoln already freed the slaves."

"Maybe they just learned about it since the slaves couldn't read back then," offered Moose.

As funny as that was, Don knew it was not true.

"They're dumb, but not that dumb," said Don.

I disagreed. I thought they were that dumb and then some. My mention of the Emancipation Proclamation reminded me of Abraham Lincoln and what Uncle Lou always said about him.

"Ol' turn-coat Abe Lincoln was a traitor to his race and to the country." Uncle Lou never mentioned Lincoln's name unless he prefaced it with an adjective that described how despicable Lincoln was in his sight, "turn-coat Abe Lincoln," was his favorite.

On my way home I couldn't help but wonder why the Negroes were so jubilant. When I got to the apartment, I found out.

Uncle Lou was pacing back and forth in our little apartment. And boy! Was he fuming! Uncle Lou hadn't had a drink since he enlisted in the Navy, but he looked like he surely could use one. Something told me that whatever the Negroes had been cheering about at school had a lot to do with why Uncle Lou was so terribly angry. I was right.

"Don't ever say the word 'baseball' in my presence again, you hear me?" he said, still pacing the floor.

"What did baseball do to you?" I casually asked.

Fire came out of his eyes. "I told you not to say that word!"

I waited, patiently.

Finally, he said, "Those dang-blasted Brooklyn Dodgers went and signed a nigger on the team. Here we have thousands of well-qualified White men who are just waiting to get on a big league team and what do they do? They hire a jigaboo."

The Negro's name was Jackie Robinson. After he got on the Dodger's baseball team, the Negroes around the school began walking with their heads held a little higher as if they'd done something special themselves.

Jackie Robinson did more than just break the color barrier in baseball; he began to speak out whenever and wherever he could be heard, railing against housing discrimination or any kind of discrimination. He complained about the Jim Crow Laws—the laws that separated Whites from Blacks in the South. Once when "Moose" and I were sitting around listening to the radio, Robinson came on, once again talking about how Negroes were being treated in the United States.

"I wish that nigger would just shut up and play ball," I exclaimed.

"Moose" looked at me, laughing. "You're becoming your Uncle Lou," he mused.

He said it with a smile on his face, but he was dead serious, and I realized that he was right. After all, I had spent most of my life with Uncle Lou, ever since I was ten years old. Of course, his views would influence mine, but that didn't bother me at all because I believed his views were right and I did not doubt for one minute his hatred of the Negro race was perfectly justified.

Uncle Lou and I didn't go to baseball games anymore, no matter what team was playing. He kept reminding me that I picked the right sport—swimming.

Swimming remained my passion in the Navy, at Wright Junior College, and at the University of Illinois where I majored in Physical Education. I had been competing in swimming meets throughout high school and college, so winning gold, silver, and bronze medals at the University of Illinois in Champaign was nothing out of the ordinary.

I still held my racist beliefs regarding Black people. The U of I had a great swimming pool, and I spent a lot of time in it; not just as part of my Physical Education curriculum, but also when I wasn't in any of my other classes. One day I was enjoying a leisurely swim when I heard a big "splash" in the water. Someone had jumped in behind me. I was backstroke swimming as usual, and I didn't bother to turn to see who my fellow swimmer was. When I got to the end of the pool and turned to go back, I saw, to my shock and horror, the other person in the water was a Negro. I didn't know I could get out of the water so fast. The coach happened to be coming into the pool area, and he noticed my quick exit.

"You jumped out of the water mighty fast, George. What's going on? You acted like you had seen a ghost."

"I did, I saw a spook," I said this practically under my breath.

"What?"

I didn't dare repeat myself. "Spook" is another name we used to label Black people. For some reason, I didn't think the Coach would appreciate that description, so I just said,

"Coach, you didn't see that Negro over there, swimming in our pool?"

"George, he has every right to be in the pool. Do you have any idea who he is?"

"I know he's a Negro."

"That Negro happens to be one of the University's top swimmers, an amazing backstroke swimmer."

Before I could say anything else, the Coach waved at the Negro, and then walked away, shaking his head in disbelief at my blatant bigotry.

I stood there, confused and conflicted. I heard the Coach's words, but they went against everything I had been taught. Adolph Kiefer was a top backstroke swimmer–he was White. Johnny Weissmuller was an excellent swimmer—he was White. Negroes were brainless, shiftless, lazy, and afraid of the water. How could I piece together everything from those last few minutes that would make enough sense for me to believe one of those people was a top backstroke swimmer? Uncle Lou would probably say, "That Nigger-loving Coach just made up that lie so he wouldn't get reported for letting a nigger in the pool." Satisfied that what Uncle Lou would probably have said was most likely right, I left the pool area to get dressed. I didn't know how long that Negro would be hogging the pool, but I wasn't about to wait to find out.

CHAPTER 6

On My Own

"What lies behind you and what lies in front of you,
pales in comparison to what lies inside of you."
–RALPH WALDO EMERSON

The U.S. Navy and four years of college prepared me to be a man. When I finally graduated from college, I knew it was time to strike out on my own. Making a career choice wasn't going to be hard. From the day I first ventured into the water as an eight-year-old at St. Bede's Summer Camp, swimming was all I ever wanted to do. It was my life, my passion, and there was never any doubt that whatever I did with the rest of my life, whatever career I chose, it would somehow involve swimming.

Some of my friends and associates from Wright Junior College and the University of Illinois didn't have a clue as to what they were going to do with their lives following school. Others were pursuing traditional careers; teachers and attorneys headed the list. As for me, I had no interest in the regular jobs.

Before I made my decision, I had gone to the library, spoke to my swim coach, and studied to find every job in existence that would somehow involve spending the greater part of my workday in the water. I finally settled on two choices—either a physical education instructor or a water polo instructor.

I fully expected Uncle Lou to be very pleased with my choices. After all, when I had announced at the age of eight that I wanted to be a famous swimmer, it was Uncle Lou who commended me for my choice, noting that I wouldn't have to be around a bunch of Negroes since they don't swim. That hadn't changed. The only Negroes I had ever known to swim were those I taught in the Navy and the Negro in the pool at the University of Illinois.

Uncle Lou didn't respond to my announcement like I thought he would.

"Are you sure that's what you want to do?" he asked.

"I've always been sure," I told him. Then I asked, "Would you rather I tried to play baseball with Jackie Robinson?"

"That wouldn't be a bad idea," he laughed, "since you can't swing a bat, maybe you'd accidently hit that nigger upside his head."

We laughed, but I still didn't understand why he wasn't excited about my career choice. "You know, Uncle Lou, you told me swimming was an excellent choice because I wouldn't have to be around a bunch of Negroes," I reminded him.

"Did I say Negroes?" he asked, surprised.

"Well, no. You said the other word that Grandma used to say wasn't nice." Strangely, for some reason I was beginning to have a hard time saying nigger. And back in those days, political correctness wasn't trending, so I don't know what it was.

Uncle Lou laughed again and then he got serious. Since he had stopped drinking, although he was still as racist as ever, he seemed to have become a little more thoughtful.

"You don't base a major decision like what you're going to do with the rest of your life on whether you'll be near Negroes," he said. "Hell, they're popping up all over the place anyway. Pretty soon you won't be able to go anyplace in life without running into one. So what you need to figure out is what kind of job pays the best salary."

I nodded my head, understanding. "So, a physical education teacher would probably make a lot more than a water polo instructor," I said.

Uncle Lou shook his head, "That's not what I meant. I'll tell you what; I'm going to let you make an intelligent decision on your own. Tomorrow, go down to the public library and ask the librarian for a listing of careers and the salary that goes with each one. Then you decide which way you want to go."

At St. Matthews, some of our field trips consisted of visiting the public library. That's when I learned to love it, and the public library still remains one of my favorite places. I was at the library bright and early the following day. I approached the librarian's desk and told her I needed a list of all the jobs in the U.S. and their corresponding salaries. "Oh, that's easy," she said. She pushed her chair back, stood up and went to a shelf where she pulled down a large book, laid it on the copy machine and copied about twenty pages.

Finally, she handed me the Xeroxed copies with every career from A to Z, showing the starting salaries and incremental salaries for each job. I immediately turned to the W's and looked up water polo instructor. I didn't expect the Water Polo instructor's salary to be way up there, but I certainly didn't expect it to be as low as it was. Assuming I was right about physical education teachers making a better salary, I turned to the P's. Teacher's salaries were not much higher than the Water Polo instructor's, and of all the teaching jobs, the Physical Education teacher was way down near the poverty level. I quickly ran my fingers down all of the pages, reading only the salaries at the far right, while looking for the largest ones.

Many salaries were much more lucrative than those of the instructors, but when I got to the S's, there was one salary that stood out above the others. Sales! The salaries for salesmen topped just about every other career, with the exception of doctors, lawyers, scientists and others that called for a lot more education than I had.

Salesmen's salaries were commission-based, meaning you had to be a really super salesman to earn the most lucrative salary. That didn't bother me at all. My two great role models in the selling industry, Uncle Lou and Uncle "Husk" taught me enough about sales to insure my success.

Uncle "Husk" had been pretty much forced out of the music business by Jimmy Petrillo, so he developed a hair care product and put his sales' skills to work. I watched him draw a crowd and keep their attention, as he talked about the new miracle ingredient called Lanolin, which was in LaGren Shampoo. (LaGren was his wife's maiden name.) When Uncle "Husk" gave his sales pitch, explaining to women why their hair was their crowning glory and LaGren Shampoo would keep them beautiful and keep their husbands smiling, they lined up by the dozens to buy his product.

As for Uncle Lou, he had come up with a great way to sell Parker Pens. A lot of people just didn't understand how to fill those pens with ink, so he created a display with a hand plunging the pen into the ink and filling it. It worked. His counter display sold a lot of Parker Pens. I had watched both of my uncles and I felt I understood the art of selling very well.

I left the library and made a beeline for our apartment. I couldn't wait to see my uncle's face when I told him my decision.

"Uncle Lou, I changed my mind. I don't want to be a physical education instructor or a water polo instructor," I said before he got a chance to even ask what I had learned at the library

"Why not?" he asked, as if he didn't know.

I showed him the documents the librarian had given me. Pointing out the salaries of teachers, and water polo instructors and then the much larger salaries of salesmen, I said, "They don't make very much money; so, I think I'll be a salesman, like you and Uncle 'Husk."

Uncle Lou took the papers and read over them for a few seconds. Then he looked at me and smiled. "You know what, George?" he said, "I think you made a good choice. And I believe you're going to make one helluva good salesman."

Uncle Lou let me think I had come to that realization all by myself. Years later it occurred to me that he had orchestrated things in a way that would bring me to the conclusion he desired without my knowing I had just bought into his decision.

If there's one thing I learned from my father and my uncles, besides salesmanship, it was how to dress the part. Clean white shirt, nicely pressed suit, nice tie, and shined shoes. I was ready to face the world. The "Help Wanted" section of the newspaper had plenty of sales jobs. I picked three or four that appeared to be the most lucrative. Being bright and early and professionally dressed got me in the front door—but that's about as far as I got.

"May I help you?"

"I saw your ad for a salesman, and I'd like to apply for the job."

"Great! What kind of sales experience have you had?"

"Well, none actually—but I know how to sell."

"Sorry, we're looking for experienced salesmen."

The answer was the same everywhere I went. After a couple of days of being rejected because of my youth and lack of sales experience, I realized getting a job in sales was not going to be as easy as I thought. Once again, I turned to my Uncle Lou. His advice: "Keep trying. Rome wasn't built in a day." I wanted to say that I wasn't trying to build Rome. I was just trying to get a job, but I knew better than to get smart with Uncle Lou. Even though I was grown, he would quickly remind me I wasn't that grown.

"O'Hare's are not quitters," he reminded me, "Now get out there and get that job."

Back to the "help wanted" ads. The *Chicago Sun-Times* published an ad saying that Sears, Roebuck and Company was hiring. What stood out in the ad were three magic words, "No experience necessary." It wasn't like I was looking at the ad for the first time. I had seen it when I first began to search the want ads, but I skipped over it, because I wasn't too keen on working at any retail store, especially Sears. My grandmother used to shop at Sears, Roebuck and Company for everything, and she would always drag me along. Boy, did I hate those shopping trips! We'd walk around Sears for hours, looking at those ugly green walls, which Sears was known for in those days. Sears was the last place I wanted to work, but they were the only ones that didn't require previous experience. So, I decided I'd just have to put up with the ugly green walls. At least I'd get some much-needed sales experience, and then I would move onto bigger and better opportunities, I reasoned.

The ad was for the Sears store at 63rd and Halsted on Chicago's South Side. I knew about the Sears on Homan Avenue, which is where Grandma shopped, but I was not familiar with that Sears or anything else on the Southside of Chicago.

"That's the Englewood community," Uncle Lou said when I told him the address; "Lots and lots of Negroes live in that area. You'd better be careful."

His warning made me more than a little nervous. Coming from an all-White grammar school, an all-White high school (except for Podgy Simmons), a mostly-White Navy experience, and two predominately White colleges, I couldn't imagine myself being in a situation with "lots and lots of Negroes." To tell the truth, that was in the early 1950's, and African Americans only made up eleven percent of the Englewood community's total population; but to Uncle Lou, eleven percent was a lot.

The next morning, I rose earlier than usual. Tying my tie, I looked myself squarely in the mirror and said, "Okay, George, the best way to convince them that you're a super salesman is by selling yourself." I remembered my Uncle "Husk's" words—"always be positive." I took the bus to 63rd Street and then I transferred and took the 63rd Street bus to Halsted. The Sears store was at the corner of 63rd and Halsted. The other large department store in the Englewood Shopping Center was Wieboldt's. A huge stone building housed the Chicago City Bank and Trust Company. There were many smaller stores in the center, including Paddors, Three Sisters, and the Five-Seven-Nine Store.

As I walked through the shopping area, I kept a keen eye out for the large number of Negroes that Uncle Lou warned me about. To my relief, I saw only a very few. As I approached the Sears store, thoughts of Grandma's shopping trips and those ugly green walls kept popping up in my mind. Once inside the store, I was pleasantly surprised to see that the walls were no longer green and ugly, and most importantly, there was not a Negro in sight—not one.

The Personnel Manager interviewed me; then I was introduced to, the store manager, who hired me on the spot. My first assignment was to sell the *American People's Encyclopedia*. My job was to convince consumers that purchasing these high-priced books was well worth the investment; especially if they had children. I put my heart into each sale, using every tactic I had learned from Uncle "Husk" and Uncle Lou. It paid off; I sold a lot of books, knowing that they would probably end up collecting dust in someone's living room or den. It occurred to me that I wouldn't have been as successful if there had been "lots and lots of Negroes" in the store, as Uncle Lou had predicted. Selling encyclopedias to people who couldn't read, and couldn't afford them would have been challenging for even the best salesman, I thought.

I forgot about my plans to gain some experience at Sears and then move on to other kinds of sales positions. Sears was a great place to work, and I made a lot of money selling on commission, so I decided to stay there. My managers could tell I was going places in the company.

"Save your money, George, because when you start getting promotions, you'll need it," they'd say.

"Why is that?"

"Managers don't make commissions like salespeople do. At first, your paycheck is going to be a lot smaller than it was when you were on commission."

That was a crucial piece of advice, since, in those days, a good salesperson could earn twice as much in commissions as a manager would make in salary. However, as you continued to get promoted up the ladder, the management salary would soon top the salary of even the highest paid commissioned salesman.

CHAPTER 7

Love, Marriage and Sears

"Not until I felt your sunshine did I realize that I had been in the shade."
–SUZY KASSEM

Besides the great pay, I discovered that my nine-to-five schedule still afforded me time to enjoy my first love, which was swimming. I still enjoyed the swim competitions, and when I wasn't working, I was getting in shape for the one-hundred-meter backstroke and the nine-mile long distance backstroke race. I would swim four miles a day on my back, from Oak Street Beach to North Avenue Beach. The great thing about backstroke swimming was that instead of looking down at the water, I could look up at the sky, the beautiful scenery, the buildings, the beach, and the people.

North Avenue Beach is in Chicago's Lincoln Park community. It's probably one of Chicago's most famous beaches, because of its great beach house and other amenities that most Chicago beaches don't have. On one particular day when I was backstroke swimming past North Avenue Beach, I noticed a very beautiful young blonde woman sitting on the beach by herself. Something compelled me to get out of the water and get a better look. The closer I got, the more beautiful she appeared. Her blonde hair highlighted the prettiest sky-blue eyes I had ever seen. Her features were perfect; her sweet smile was enchanting. As I stood over her, staring, she looked up with a puzzled expression on her face. I suppose I should have said something, but although I was talkative and outgoing as a salesman, I was bashful in situations like this. After staring at her long enough to keep a mental picture of her in my mind, I left to swim back to the Oak Street Beach.

The next day, as I was backstroking I looked over at the same spot, and once again I saw her, sitting and looking out at the water. Again I felt compelled to come out of the water and get a better look. I don't' know what was going on in her mind as I stood there, silently looking at her. I wanted to say something, but no words would come out of my mouth. She broke the ice.

"You're coming back to see me again." It was more of a statement than a question.

"Yes," I agreed.

Hearing my voice coming out of my mouth unlocked all the words that seemed stuck in my head. Here I was this bashful guy who had never thought about girls before, telling this gorgeous blonde how beautiful she was. I told her my name and how much I loved to swim, especially the backstroke; I told her I was a salesman at Sears, Roebuck and Company. She smiled, listening to my words attentively as I went through my narrative. I was thrilled. This lovely blonde, with enchanting blue eyes, was interested in what I had to say.

She told me her name was Jean Kloss, and she was a Bell Telephone Company employee, and like me, she was a Catholic. Best of all, she loved to swim. It was almost too good to be true. She was everything I wanted in a woman. A Catholic who loved to swim! I only had one concern —although she was Catholic, she wasn't Irish. How was I going toexplain that to my racist Uncle Lou? How could I tell him I met a beautiful woman, and I'm in love for the first time in my life, but she's Polish—German-Polish to be exact?

As this was going on in my mind, I realized I was way ahead of myself. I just met this woman and already I was thinking of introducing her to my family. I hadn't even mustered up the courage to ask her for a date.

"Did you walk here?" I asked her.

"No, I rode my bike," she said.

"That's great; I rode my bike, too."

I asked her to wait until I went to my locker to change clothes, which I did at record speed. I dashed out of the beach house half expecting her to be gone. She was still there. She waited for me! I was ecstatic! We continued riding our bikes to the beach and back home together almost every day. It was easy to have a conversation with Jean; we talked about everything under the sun and found out we had a lot in common.

After a few weeks, I finally got up the nerve to ask her out to dinner. It took a little longer for me to muster up the courage to finally say, "I'd like you to meet my Uncle Lou. He's a marketing genius and a great guy. You'd like him. He loves everybody, except Negroes and Jews." She laughed and agreed, "Nobody likes them. Your Uncle Lou sounds a lot like my father."

I met her parents. She was right, her father and Uncle Lou were a lot alike, especially when it came to hating Negroes. She had experienced that same kind of racist upbringing that I had, which was another thing we had in common. I brought her to meet Uncle Lou and I could see he was impressed. When I came back to the apartment after taking Jean home, Uncle Lou was still up.

"Tell me that girl's name again," he said.

"Jean," I told him.

"Jean who?" he asked.

"Kloss, Jean Kloss."

He thought about that for a minute, then said,

"Kloss? What kind of name is Kloss? What kind of name is Kloss?" Before I could answer, he answered himself.

"Polish. The girl is Polish. You couldn't find yourself a nice Irish girl?"

I didn't say anything.

Finally, he said, "She's a sweet girl, and beautiful, too. You did alright, George."

I breathed a sigh of relief. Uncle Lou approved.

Jean and I started spending more time together. The first time I asked her to marry me, she said, "I don't know about that." I didn't press her. We remained friends. We'd go bike riding or swimming or to lunch or dinner together. She met Uncle "Husk" and Aunt Vivian, and they liked her immediately. Why wouldn't they? There was nothing about Jean Kloss not to like. She had the kind of personality that immediately drew people to her.

We were out to dinner one day when she said, "George, my father is very enthused about you." Wow! That meant the world to me, and it was the turning point in our relationship. Shortly afterward, I asked Jean to marry me again. This time she said yes. I think her father's approval of me had a lot to do with her acceptance.

Jean and I were married in St. Ferdinand's Catholic Church. We had planned to drive to Jackson, Tennessee, and then to Florida for our honeymoon, but my car had other plans. It was an old car I had bought used. Like most used cars, it decided to break down right before our honeymoon. I didn't know what to do. Somehow flying just didn't seem as romantic and plus it was very expensive. Jean agreed and said we could wait and have a honeymoon later. I hated to put it off, but Jean made sense. Just as I was about to tell her I believed she was right, the doorbell rang. It was my good friend, Ron Orr.

"Came by to wish you guys a happy honeymoon," Ron said.

He gave me a box of brownies his wife had baked so we'd have something to snack on while we were on the road.

"We'll take the brownies," I told him, "But we'll probably eat them here. The honeymoon is off for a little while."

At first, Ron thought I was joking. He knew how much Jean and I were looking forward to getting away. I explained that the car made the decision for us. It decided to shut down, and there was nothing we could do about it.

Ron listened, and said, "I'll see you later."

I figured he could tell that Jean and I were both a little disappointed, and I guessed he didn't feel comfortable participating in our pity party.

Thirty minutes later Ron showed up. He was driving one car, and his wife was driving the other.

"I had to bring her along because I couldn't drive two cars," Ron explained. Then he gave me the keys to his brand new car.

His wife said, "I didn't bake those brownies for you to sit at home and eat them; you're supposed to eat them on your road trip."

I couldn't ask for a better friend. Ron just passed away recently, and I miss him very much.

Needless to say, Jean and I were overjoyed. We'd be able to take that road trip to Jackson, Tennessee, after all—and in the comfort of a luxurious new car.

We had a great honeymoon. We had planned to go to Florida also, but the weather was too hot. After honeymooning in Jackson, we headed back to Chicago.

When Jean told me she was pregnant, I was hoping for a son. We planned on having more than one child, and we both felt that the son should come first so he could take care of his little sister. God answered my prayer. We named our first-born son, George III. When Jean became pregnant again, we were so sure it was a girl, we only thought of girl's names. But it was another boy, who we named Bob.

After Bob was born, I insisted that Jean stay at home to be a full-time mother. She agreed. Sears was paying me a decent amount of money, and we did very well on my salary alone.

By the time my third son, Michael, was born, our West Side neighborhood was undergoing a tremendous change. The Negroes, who used to stay in their place when I was a youth, were now invading our community in droves. They were everywhere. You couldn't walk down the street or walk into a store without seeing at least one, usually two, or even three of them. Negroes were even enrolling in the previously all-White schools. Jean and I agreed that it was time to move.

My mind went back to my third-grade classroom at St. Matthews. I thought about how traumatic it was to have one Negro in my classroom. I didn't want my children to go through what I went through or worse. At St. Matthews they sent the little Negro boy home. Now, it was too many Negroes in the schools in our community. Sending one home would not make a difference, and they certainly couldn't put them all out.

We found a home in Hinsdale, a small community with only fifty-five families, and not one Negro or Jew or minority of any kind.

Uncle Lou was a frequent and welcome guest at our dinner table. He loved everything about our new house, especially the lily-White neighborhood. "You were smart to get your family away from those niggers," he would say. He had long stopped drinking, but he was still ranting and raving about the "niggers and Jews," and Grandma wasn't there to say, "Don't say nigger say, Negro." Jean would never correct him because that word was as familiar to her as it was to me. Neither one of us saw anything wrong with it.

Racism had a prominent place in almost everything that happened in those days, but it was such a regular part of the life I lived that I never thought of myself, my friends, or everyday situations as being racist.

Harry Truman had just won re-election as the President of the United States when I began working at Sears. Although one couldn't call him a "liberal," he did advocate fair treatment of all people regardless of race. Truman signed a law making it mandatory to treat all Civil Service employees equally. He also established a Committee on Government Contract Compliance to reassure that any company that dealt with the Federal Government or supplied weapons or any equipment to the military had to have a policy of equality toward minorities.

As a major supplier to the armed forces, Sears adopted an equal employment opportunity policy, on paper. Negroes were welcome to come into Sears and apply for jobs or credit. When they did, we would treat them cordially; fill out the job or credit application, and place a big "X" in the corner of the application as a signal to everyone that the applicant was a Negro. Accordingly, the reviewing employee would place all the requests with an "X" into the "circular file," which was our nickname for the wastebasket. Some of the employment applications wound up in the regular files, but the "X" in the corner reminded anyone looking through those files that there should be no action taken on those particular documents. I followed this procedure faithfully; making sure my "X" was large enough to get noticed.

Not very many Negroes applied for jobs at Sears and even fewer shopped there. Though Englewood was quickly becoming a mixed neighborhood, most Blacks patronized South Center, a large Negro department store on 47th Street, in the community called Bronzeville. The few times I did see a Black person in Sears, it was usually a Black woman pushing a White baby in a stroller.

I worked hard at Sears, and it paid off. My promotions came quickly, from selling encyclopedias to selling washing machines, refrigerators, and televisions. Later, I was invited to be in the Sears' Executive Training Program for Management, after which I became Division Manager, then Merchandising Manager, then head of all appliances for Sears. I loved teaching my managers the art of getting a customer's attention, demonstrating our great products, and then closing the sale.

By the 1960's, the Negro population had soared, from eleven percent in 1950 to twenty-two percent according to the 1960 Census. I didn't need to read the Census numbers to know about the change. Negroes began shopping at Sears. They were buying the top of the line items; and according to our policy, a Sears employee had to go to the home and demonstrate any new appliance delivered to any home, even a Negro's home.

The experience of going into one of those homes was even more astonishing than when Uncle Lou used to take me to the Negro homes east of Sacramento Boulevard where he collected rent. Those people had exquisite tastes, expensive furniture, and their homes were immaculate.

The first time I visited a Negro's home to demonstrate a Sears' product; when I got home I told Jean,

"I went into a Negro's home today."

Jean was sympathetic, "I guess now that more of them are moving into that area, going into their homes is part of your job."

"I didn't mind that," I explained, "But I was surprised their houses were so clean."

Jean thought about it for a minute and then offered an entirely logical explanation.

"That's because most of them clean White people's houses for a living; so of course, the White people would teach them how to clean." That's how White people explained those things in the era of segregation.

"But their furniture is so beautiful and expensive-looking." I would say.

"Really!" Jean's eyes got big just like Grandma's when I told her about the couches and tables and chairs. "George, are you making this up?"

"No, really," I insisted.

Jean thought about it. "Maybe the White people they worked for gave them the furniture."

A more sinister thought rose up in my mind, *maybe they stole it*. I didn't share that with Jean because it didn't make sense. If they were stealing furniture, why would they shop at Sears, buying expensive appliances? Plus, even though they were Black, they still didn't seem like the type to steal furniture.

Jean didn't have any more explanations, so we ended the conversation there. We concluded the one or two homes I had gone into were those of exceptional Negroes and the others would look just like we expected–dirty, no furniture, with dirty kids running around in dirty clothes and even eating off the dirty floors. Even though I continued demonstrating our appliances in the homes of Negroes and never came across a filthy house that had no furniture, I still held the belief that these few Negroes were the exception. I was sure the masses of Negroes were living in dirty homes without furniture, with dirty little children running around, while the parents shuffled back and forth, rolling their eyes like Stepin Fetchit.

Eventually, I was promoted to Merchandise Manager for all Sears' appliances. Sears had just gotten into the business of selling 45-RPM records and record albums. These products also became part of my responsibility, as well as selecting, buying, and advertising the albums and 45-RPM records for Sears.

CHAPTER 8

The Jaycees & a Hoodlum Priest

"We believe: That faith in God gives meaning and purpose to human life; that the brotherhood of man transcends the sovereignty of nations; that economic justice can best be won by free men through free enterprise; that government should be of laws rather than of men; that earth's great treasure lies in human personality; and that service to humanity is the best work of life.
–The Jaycee Creed

In those days, Corporate America took on the responsibility of being the harvester of the future leaders of America. No one took that responsibility more seriously than Gordon Metcalfe, the Chicago District Manager of Sears. If Mr. Metcalf saw an employee who seemed to have promise, he would make it his personal mission to groom that employee to not only benefit Sears but also to help the community. I am grateful that I was fortunate enough to be one of the lucky ones in whom Mr. Metcalfe took a personal interest. Without

Mr. Metcalf watching and overseeing my ascension up the Sears ladder and giving me great advice and counseling along the way, I might not have enjoyed such a successful career.

He would often stop by my station and ask me how everything was going. One day he called me into his office, I knew it must have been something important.

"How do you like working for Sears, George?"

"I like it fine," I said.

"Well, you're doing a fantastic job for us. Now, I'd like to see you put some of the same kind of energy into serving the community."

I wasn't sure I understood exactly what he was talking about, so he explained further.

"You've done such a great job of demonstrating your leadership skills here at Sears; I'd like you to join the Junior Chamber of Commerce, where you can put those skills to work for the communities.

I had no idea what the Junior Chamber of Commerce was, so I sat in Mr. Metcalfe's office for over an hour as he explained. It was an organization for young men between the ages of twenty-one and thirty-five, formed for the express purpose of helping their members become tomorrow's leaders. He said they were called the Jaycees for short and their leadership-training program had produced some of the world's most successful business and professional men, as well as mayors, governors, Congressmen, Senators, and leaders, not just in the United States, but in many of the countries throughout the world.

It sounded good, but I thought about my wife, Jean, and my three sons, George, Bob, and Mike. I was spending enough time away from them as it was because I still swam after work when the weather was pleasant. I couldn't imagine spending even more time away from home.

"Does being a member of the Jaycees mean I'd have to attend a lot of meetings?" I asked.

"You can attend as many meetings or as few as you want to. It's up to you," he assured me.

I could tell from the conversation that asking me was just a courtesy and, in so many words, Mr. Metcalfe was telling me that he was expecting me to join the Jaycees and even hinting that my future growth at Sears depended on it.

I swallowed my misgivings and stood up to shake Mr. Metcalfe's hand. "I'd be honored to become a member of the Jaycees," I said. Mr. Metcalfe had a similar look of pride in his eyes like Uncle Lou would have when he tousled my hair. However, Mr. Metcalfe didn't tousle my hair; instead, he pumped my hand over and over while patting me on the back. "You're going to go places, O'Hare," he said. "Mark my word."

Mr. Metcalfe gave me a book entitled *Young Men Can Change the World*, by Booton Herndon, which explained this phenomenon called the Junior Chamber of Commerce. I read the book over and over. I was particularly struck by one passage:

> "*Thousands of young men have found their wildest ambitions realized through the Junior Chamber. This movement has changed the lives of more young men and with more dramatic impact than any other similar organization in the history of mankind. Working in, for, and with the Junior Chamber can, it has been proved; turn a tongue-tied young rube into a poised executive, an assembly-line worker into a multi-millionaire, a so-called egghead into a pragmatic politician.*"

In 1960, according to Booton Herndon, the Jaycees in the United States numbered 200,000; average age, thirty; yearly income, $6,000 ($6,000 was a decent salary in those days). Herndon also said, "The typical Jaycee, the young man who is going somewhere in the world, finds joy in work, a thrill in accomplishment."

I am so glad Mr. Metcalf forced me to join the Jaycees because that's when I started meeting people I never would have met in my life.

A significant portion of the Jaycee's training program consisted of listening to motivational speakers. Members were encouraged to listen to tape recordings or radio broadcasts. I learned the best way to experience those phenomenal speakers was to see and hear them in person.

The Jaycees gave me an appreciation for motivational and spiritual speakers. Sears would supply the tickets for Jaycee members to attend speeches and lectures by speakers that were renown in those days. Dr. Norman Vincent Peale, Zig Ziglar, and Dale Carnegie stood out as the greatest speakers. Just listening to Dale Carnegie's seminars on "How to win friends and influence people" helped me overcome my shyness.

Reverend Billy Graham was an evangelist on a mission to bring souls to Christ. To me, he was not only bringing people to Christ, but he was also teaching people how to live. Too many of us have been taught how to make a living, but not how to live. The world could use more Billy Graham's.

Listening to those speakers was not enough for me. Whenever I had the opportunity, I would go up to them afterward, introduce myself and shake their hands. I was impressed by their warmth and friendliness and willingness to answer questions and give advice. The great Dr. Norman Vincent Peale took the time to tell me some ways in which I could become a better salesman and he even gave me tips on how to master the art of closing the deal. Even though I thought I knew all that from watching and listening to Uncle Lou and Uncle "Husk," I was always open to good advice and new techniques.

Billy Graham met with the Jaycees so often that he got to know me by name. These weren't the only speakers I followed. I became a speaker "groupie." Anytime I heard someone was speaking, I'd make it my business to be there, no matter how famous or obscure they were. Most of the seminars cost money and Sears was excellent about purchasing tickets. All I had to do was ask.

The Chicago Junior Chamber of Commerce was not just a social organization that only had meetings, dinners and fundraisers and listened to speakers. Every Jaycee member also had to have an area of community service for which he was responsible.

I attended trainings and listened to the speakers, but I had yet to identify the area of community service in which I would volunteer. Then one day, the Jaycees had a convention and the keynote speaker was a Catholic Jesuit Priest named Father Charles "Dismas" Clark. People called him the "hoodlum priest," mainly because he spoke in the thuggish vernacular, like a character from a James Cagney film. He took the middle name of "Dismas" after the thief on the cross at

Jesus' crucifixion. His mission was to get the world to understand that prisoners were decent people who had just gotten caught up in adverse circumstances; and given a chance; they could be rehabilitated back into society. I had never thought about prisoners in that way, but Father "Dimas' presentation made me re-think everything I had been led to believe about them.

After his speech, I rushed up to the podium and introduced myself. I wanted to hear more from this man and asked him when and where he would be speaking again. He was receptive and down-to-earth, explaining he lived in St. Louis, but came to Chicago from time-to-time. "Take my phone number," he said, handing me a slip of paper, "and let's keep in touch."

Oh, did we ever stay in touch! Father "Dismas" Clark became my mentor, advisor, and friend. Because of Father "Dismas," I finally identified my area of service. I became the founder and chairman of the Prisoner and Ex-Prisoner Rehabilitation Program of the Chicago Junior Chamber of Commerce.

During my frequent visits to prisons, I also met a wonderful man by the name of Warden Jack Johnson of the Cook County Jail. Johnson was known to be tough, but he was also a very good person and treated the inmates fairly. "I've never broken a promise to an inmate," he once said, "and I never will." Warden Johnson truly believed in the rehabilitation of prisoners. He always complained about the unfair way in which they were treated. "They do their time," he would say. "They should have a chance to get back into society, but the question is who will hire them, so they don't end up right back in jail?"

After visiting the inmates, Father "Dismas" and I would go back into Warden Johnson's office where he kept his stash of liquor for visitors. On one of those visits he said,

"You know, George, you're in a position to do a lot for the ex-convicts."

I agreed with him. "You mean as Chairman of the Prisoner and Ex-Prisoner Rehabilitation Committee?"

"No, no, I mean as an executive at Sears, Roebuck and Company. That's a big company, and I'm sure they've got enough room for a couple of ex-convicts."

I thought about it. "I guess I could talk to management," I said, "But I'm not sure I'd be convincing."

"I'm sure Father Dismas would," said the Warden.

I made an appointment to talk to Mr. Metcalf. After all, he got me into the Jaycees, so he should want to know what I was doing with the organization. Mr. Metcalf had his secretary set up a meeting between the Sears management, Father Dismas, and Warden Jackson. Father "Dismas" made a compelling argument. "How many of you need a better salesman?" Hands went up throughout the room. Then he made his case: "If you want a good salesperson, hire an ex-con. Anyone who has the guts to put a gun in their pocket, then walk up to a gas station manager and say, 'this is a stick-up, give me all your money,' would make a great salesperson, because selling takes guts." The managers were cautiously nodding their heads in agreement. By the end of the meeting, most of the managers agreed to give some ex-convicts a chance. Of course, all the ex-convicts they hired were White. They would not even hire a Black college graduate with a doctor's degree, so how could I dare ask them to hire a Black ex-con?

As Chairman of the Prisoner and Ex-Prisoner Rehabilitation Committee, I helped raise funds for rehabilitation centers or halfway houses Negroes were in the minority everywhere except in prisons. Most prisons were predominately Negro, which meant many of the businessmen from whom I solicited donations were also Negroes. I would usually meet with those entrepreneurs and Father "Dismas" at a downtown restaurant whenever he was in town. I was committed to the cause, but not committed enough to venture into the South Side of Chicago. Uncle Lou had already warned me not to ever go to the South Side—especially at night. He said Negroes carried razors, and they would rob any White person who would dare set foot in their neighborhood after dark. In spite of all the lectures, seminars and motivational speeches I had attended, there was nothing I heard that could cause me to stop believing everything Uncle Lou told me about the Negroes and the Jews.

CHAPTER 9

Trouble-Making Preacher

"It is easy to forget that in his day, King was considered a dangerous troublemaker. He was harassed by the FBI and vilified in the media."
—Peter Dreier

By the mid-1950's, Negroes were becoming more vocal in demanding their rights. There were all-White schools and all-Black schools, especially in the South, and Negroes argued that the all-Black schools didn't have the funding, resources or teachers to give their students a decent education. Organizations like the NAACP and the Urban League were demanding that Negroes receive the fair treatment that was guaranteed by the Constitution. Around that time, Thurgood Marshall won the famous Brown vs. Board of Education case, which led to integration of the public schools.

One day, one of my co-workers asked me if I had heard about the killing of a Negro boy named Emmett Till. I had not, so he told me the gruesome details. "He must have done something pretty bad," I mused. "Yeah," my co-worker replied, "He whistled at a White woman. They think it might have been her husband that killed him." "I don't blame him," I found myself saying as my co-worker looked at me in disbelief. "I mean, I don't blame him for being angry," I said, envisioning what I would do if I ever caught a Negro whistling at Jean, "But he didn't have to kill that boy."

That killing brought more attention to the struggle of Negroes and the southern Jim Crow laws than the Urban League and the NAACP combined had been able to muster. To make matters worse, around that same time a Negro woman by the name of Rosa Parks had been arrested for not getting up and giving a White man her seat on a bus in Montgomery, Alabama.

All of this might have died down eventually had it not been for a Negro who called himself Reverend Dr. Martin Luther King, Jr. He helped arrange and then led a boycott of the entire Montgomery bus system. Negroes would walk rather than take a bus, and the bus company was losing money. "He's a Communist and a trouble-maker," Uncle Lou would say about King. I didn't know about the Communist part, but there was no doubt in my mind that he was a troublemaker.

I had learned from childhood that the best thing Negroes could do for themselves was to stay in their place. Yet, this Reverend King was encouraging Negroes to come out of their places. He was preaching that Negroes should have the same rights as White people, and that they should all be treated equally. I had never heard him speak, and had no desire to. I had heard plenty of accounts of the things he said and that was enough for me to agree with everything Uncle Lou said about him.

One evening as I was turning off the lights in my office and preparing to leave for the day, Mr. Metcalfe stopped by and asked me what I planned to do after work. I told him I planned to go home and have a nice, quiet family dinner with my wife Jean and my sons. He said there was a speaker in town and he would really like for me to go with him to hear him. Mr. Metcalfe knew how much I loved hearing good speakers. I turned the lights back on in the office and phoned Jean. She was a little disappointed to hear that I wasn't going to be home for dinner, but when I mentioned the fact that Mr. Metcalfe had invited me to hear a very important speaker, she was more understanding. She knew my relationship with Mr. Metcalfe was key to my career growth at Sears. Evidently, Mr. Metcalfe had heard of this speaker from colleagues and was anxious to hear him for himself, but he didn't want to go alone. "Where are we going?" I asked.

"To the South Side of Chicago," he replied.

I stopped dead in my tracks. Even though the Sears store was in Englewood, that was as much South Side as I was willing to experience, especially at night. Uncle Lou told me many times about how the Negroes carried knives and would attack and rob White people who came into their South Side neighborhoods.

"It's in the Hyde Park area," he continued.

I breathed a sigh of relief. I was familiar with Chicago's Hyde Park. The Jaycees had met in that area once or twice. It was about 60 percent white, and although it had a growing Negro population, most of them were in some way associated with the University of Chicago which had a large presence in that community. I insisted that I would drive my own car and meet Mr. Metcalfe there.

"Any more questions?" Mr. Metcalfe asked somewhat jokingly.

"Just one," I said, "who is the speaker?"

Mr. Metcalfe was surprised at his own oversight. "I didn't tell you?" he sincerely asked, "It's that Reverend from Montgomery Alabama, you know, King. You've heard of him."

Yes, I had heard of him and career growth or not, there is no way I would have agreed to go had I known it was him.

"That trouble maker?" I exclaimed.

"Well, I haven't heard that he was a trouble maker," Mr. Metcalfe said. Metcalfe was prejudiced, like all White people, but unlike Uncle Lou and me, he wasn't a bigot. Even though he didn't hire Negroes, he didn't hate them either.

The idea of going to hear a Negro speak, especially on my own time, was not at all appealing. I thought about all the things Uncle Lou had told me about this so-called Reverend King, "Going all over the country inciting Negroes to come out of their communities and invade our White neighborhoods." If I was going to skip dinner with my family to go to see a Negro, I would rather it had been a Stepin Fetchit movie. At least it would have given me a laugh.

I tried to hide my anger and frustration from Mr. Metcalfe as we walked in silence to the parking lot. When we got to my car, Mr. Metcalfe told me the speech was going to be at the Chicago Theological Seminary. I told him I would follow him there.

When we arrived at the Theological Seminary, the person at the security desk directed us to the lunchroom, where Dr. King's speech was just beginning. There were about twenty-five people in the audience; mostly Negroes. Mr. Metcalfe and I represented two of the four or five White people listening as King talked about equality for the Negro. He talked about fair housing and equal employment opportunity. I was determined not to like his speech, but I found myself paying attention as he gave historical perspectives and quoted biblical scriptures, making them relevant to the current situation. His analogies and metaphors helped to make everything he said understandable. I had never heard anyone speak so eloquently. By the conclusion of his speech, I had forgotten he was a Negro. I was overwhelmed!!

As we were leaving, Mr. Metcalfe asked me if I enjoyed the speech. I was able to honestly say that I did enjoy it very much. I began the thirty-mile drive to my suburban home, mulling over the things he had said. I couldn't wait to tell—who? Not Jean. I could hear her now. "Is that the important speaker? A Negro?" She couldn't phantom me missing dinner with the family to listen to a Negro give a speech. Just as I had picked up a lot of my prejudices from Uncle Lou, Jean had also grown up in a racist family, and she still held onto the beliefs her father had instilled in her mind. Uncle Lou would have thought I was out of my mind if I told him I spent an evening listening to a Negro give a speech. He was convinced that Negroes didn't have the capacity to make speeches. Uncle Lou once told me *Amos and Andy* was one of the funniest radio shows on the air, as long as there were White actors playing the characters.

"When they began to televise the show, they could no longer use White actors. They had to have real Negroes. Next thing you know, they canceled the show, probably because the Negroes didn't know how to read their lines," he said.

I later learned that the real reason for the cancellation of the show was the NAACP's objection to the way the sitcom portrayed Negroes.

No, he'd never buy the fact that a Negro could give a speech; let alone a good speech. He'd probably say, "Somebody should ask that Negro preacher what White man wrote that speech for him and who taught him how to say it. In fact, look and see if he had something in his ear so somebody could feed him his lines."

Imagining what Uncle Lou would probably say made me think, *What if Dr. King had not written that speech himself? What if a White person had written it for him, then taught him how to deliver it.* Even a dog could be trained, and Negroes were only a little bit more intelligent than dogs.

More convinced than ever that the Negro preacher could not have possibly written that speech himself, I knew the only way I could prove myself to be right was to actually hear the Negro speak, away from the podium where he could read the words of the speech and deliver it as the White man had trained him to. I turned up the little street, headed toward my home. By the time I arrived at home and let the garage door up, my curiosity had gotten the best of me. Hoping Jean hadn't seen me, I let the garage door back down without pulling the car in, turned around, and headed back to the Chicago Theological Seminary.

On the way back, I asked myself *"Why in the world would you expect this man to be in the lunchroom of the Chicago Theological Seminary almost an hour after his speech?"* Half expecting to find the building locked, or the lunchroom empty, I was pleasantly surprised to walk into the building and find Dr. King sitting at a table with a small group of people, including the other two White people who were at the speech. I sat a few tables away and waited patiently.

Finally, Dr. King stood up and the group began to disperse. He came right to my table.

"Are you waiting for me?" He asked.

"Yes," I answered, "I went all the way home and drove back thirty miles to speak with you."

"Well, this sounds like something important," he said, smiling, "What can I do for you?"

He was genuinely a nice man. There was no way I could ask him, "Which of those White people wrote that speech for you and taught you how to say it?" I was genuinely surprised that he spoke as eloquently and intelligently away from the podium as he did while delivering the speech. I found myself saying,

"I'm the Chairman of the Prisoner and Ex-Prisoner Rehabilitation Committee of the Junior Chamber of Commerce. I enjoyed your speech very much, and I'd like to invite you to come and speak to some of our inmates."

"The Jaycees," he said, "That's a good organization."

I was impressed that he knew about the Jaycees.

"What do you do besides chair that very worthwhile committee?" he asked.

"I'm the manager for Sears's advertising and their electronics merchandise," I said.

He nodded. "Well, I don't come to Chicago very often," he said, "But I can let you know when I plan to speak here again and maybe you can help promote attendance."

"I'd be happy to," I said. What was I saying? I had enough on my plate with the Chicago Jaycees and now I was volunteering to help promote this Negro? Uncle Lou would probably send me to have my head examined. Dr. King and I exchanged phone numbers.

A few weeks later, one of the Jaycee leaders mentioned they were looking for speakers. "We keep having the same speakers over and over. We need to bring a fresh, new voice to the table," he said.

"Would you like the Reverend Dr. Martin Luther King, Jr?" I asked.

He paused and looked at me. "You mean the Negro preacher?"

"You'd be surprised. Dr. King doesn't sound like an average Negro."

"Would we have to pay him?"

I knew he wouldn't have asked that question if I had proposed a White speaker. The Jaycees gave their speakers pretty sizable honorariums.

"No, I think he just wants to get his message out," I said, "But the Jaycees could pay his airfare and hotel."

He agreed to invite Dr. King to come to Chicago and speak to the organization, and I was asked to extend the invitation to him. I phoned Dr. King and told him the Jaycees wanted him to come and speak to their membership.

"There is no honorarium," I explained, "But they'll put you up in a hotel and pay your airfare."

Dr. King insisted on paying his own airfare, although he did allow the Jaycees to book him into a very nice hotel.

When Dr. King spoke to the Jaycees, his speech was just as eloquent before our all-White audience as it had been at the Chicago Theological Seminary. I watched my fellow Jaycee members become as mesmerized as I was the first time I heard him. One thing I noticed about Dr. King's speeches was that he would repeat certain phrases over and over again. It's my belief that he believed in the axiom, "repetition is the secret of all learning; the more you say it, the more it is instilled in the minds of the listeners." Dr. King was as much a teacher as he was a preacher.

After his speech, the Jaycees couldn't stop talking about what a great speaker he was.

"You were right George," they said, "Dr. King is phenomenal!"

"The next time you want him to come and speak, send him a check," I suggested.

From that time on, the Jaycees would send Dr. King a check when they wanted him to speak at a Jaycee function. His speeches were relevant, inspiring and instructional. Plus everything he said was "acceptable," which meant the press was able to print his words. As a result, the Junior Chamber of Commerce received a lot of exposure. If the headline said, "Dr. King Speaking at Junior Chamber of Commerce Event," there would be standing room only. Membership in the Jaycees increased.

Dr. King was a down-to-earth guy with a fantastic sense of humor, not at all like I had pictured a typical Negro to be. We had a great conversation on the way back to the hotel. "He's different," I thought. "I like him," I remembered Podgy Simmons and the little Negro boy that sat in the desk behind mine for one whole day at St. Matthews. I wondered if they had grown up to be as intelligent and upright as Dr. King. I thought about what my Grandmother used to say, "Those people are nice, as long as they stay in their place." Well, Dr. King fit that description, but he wasn't staying in his place, and he wasn't encouraging other Negroes to remain in their places either.

I was wishing I had the nerve to tell him that what he was doing was wrong. "You're an exception to the Negro race," I wanted to inform him, "But you're encouraging other Negroes to think they're as good as White people, and that could be dangerous." The words I wanted to say to him were in my head, but they got stuck in my throat. So, I just listened to him as he spoke about his philosophy and beliefs about equality.

The one person who wasn't happy about my relationship with Dr. King was my Uncle Lou.

"Why would you want to have anything to do with that Communist?" he'd ask me.

I stood my ground. "He's not a Communist; he's just trying to help his people."

Uncle Lou would just throw his hands up and shake his head. I guess he wondered where he had gone wrong. Perhaps he was beginning to think that all the effort he had put into teaching me to be a racist was turning out to be a waste. What Uncle Lou didn't understand was, even though I still believed everything I learned from him about Negroes; and though, for me, the Stepin Fetchit image continued to personify everything Negroes were about– shuffling, lazy, good-for-nothing—this one man was an exception. He was probably like no other Negro in the world.

I began to find out about Chambers of Commerce in different parts of the city. There were no Negroes in the Chicago Junior Chambers of Commerce, but there was a Negro Junior Chamber of Commerce chapter on the South Side of Chicago called the South End Junior Chamber of Commerce or the South End Jaycees. I met the leader of the South End Jaycees, and he invited me to attend their meetings. George Jones, the vice president and general manager of the Joe Louis Milk Company, often held meetings at his home. Even though the Joe Louis Milk Company was George Jones' business, his real passion was civil rights and the Black community. He couldn't have found a better place to protest inequality than Chicago, Illinois, which Dr. King once described as "the most segregated city in the world."

George Jones was very active in the protests and boycotts that led to the formation of Operation Breadbasket. George loved bringing people together from various backgrounds as much as he loved organizing events. Dr. King was a frequent guest speaker at his meetings.

At other times, we'd meet at the home of Dr. Herbert Odom. Dr. Odom was one of the most well-known and successful Negro dentists in Chicago. He was also an amateur boxer, who had once challenged Muhammad Ali. However, like George Jones, his number one priority was to gain justice and equality for his Negro brothers and sisters.

As they fanaticized about having the same things as Whites had, the same privileges, and being able to live in White neighborhoods, I thought of what Grandma always said, "Negroes are nice as long as they stay in their place." What would she say now, listening to these Negroes talk about leaving their places and coming into ours? Without a doubt, Uncle Lou would have had a fit if he knew these kinds of conversations were going on. As farfetched as their discussions were, I still found them fascinating.

I was intrigued by these Negroes. They had good manners, and they spoke the King's English as well as any White person. One day, I was taking Dr. King to his hotel, and I mentioned how impressed I was with the people at the meeting.

"Why were you so impressed?" he asked.

I told him I was impressed because they spoke so well and appeared to be intelligent.

"But aren't your coworkers and managers at Sears smart and don't they speak well?" he asked.

"Well, yes," I said, "But they're White."

The minute those words came out of my mouth I wanted to retract them, but Dr. King just laughed.

"George, you obviously never knew any Negroes when you were growing up."

"Sure I did," I said. Then I proceeded to tell him about the little Black kid that sat at the desk behind mine one day at St. Matthews Catholic school, and about Podgy Simmons, the Black star football player at Austin High School.

Dr. King just shook his head sadly, "That's the problem with segregation," he said, "People hate what they don't know, and segregation doesn't allow people of different races to get to know each other."

I wanted to tell him it's not what we *don't* know; it's what we *do* know. I wanted to say that he, George Jones, Dr. Odom, and the rest of the Negroes who met with them were exceptions. If all Negroes were like them, I wanted to say, then White people would have no problem welcoming them into their neighborhoods. We wouldn't mind letting them go to school with our kids. But if you want to know what most Negroes are like, just watch a Stepin Fetchit movie. Watch *Amos'n Andy* on television, or walk down a street in downtown Chicago and watch a Negro shining a White man's shoes and talking jive talk, snapping the shoeshine rag and saying, "how you like that, Boss?" I wanted to say all that, but somehow I thought that would spoil his cheerful mood. I decided just to keep it to myself and let him continue to think the only reason we didn't like Negroes was because we didn't know them.

In the spirit of taking Dr. King's advice to get to know more about Negroes, I began barhopping. There were many, many bars in the Negro neighborhoods, and having inherited my mother's love for bar-hopping, and no longer fearing Black neighborhoods (thanks to Dr. Odom's and George Jones' southside neighborhood meetings),I began to go to the various bars within the Black community . Sometimes I'd go to a bar with one of the Black people after a meeting; but I didn't mind venturing into different neighborhood bars by myself. I was on a mission. Was Dr. King right? Were the average Black people on the streets and in the bars as intelligent as the Black men and women in Dr. Odom's and George Jones' meetings? The more I discovered about Black people, the more I wanted to learn. Someone once told me the best places to find out about a community was the local bar or the church. I had no intention of going to any Black churches, so I stuck to the bars.

One night I was at a bar on Forty-Seventh and King Drive when I struck up a conversation with a man named Clarence. When you're drinking and talking in a bar, you don't exchange last names. I was George, and he was Clarence. Clarence and I talked about everything. He was impressed by the fact that I knew Dr. King. We didn't agree on everything. I was a White Sox fan; he liked the Chicago Cubs. He said the White Sox were prejudiced because they didn't have any Black players. I wanted to say, "The Dodgers have Jackie Robinson, isn't that enough?" We were in the middle of one of our friendly disagreements when the bartender called out, "Last call for alcohol."

"Say, why don't you come over to my place so we can finish this conversation?" Clarence said. "I've got a couple of drinks at the house, and you can meet my wife if she's still up." I doubted whether his wife would be up at two o'clock in the morning, but I agreed to go and have a beer or two.

Clarence's apartment was on the sixteenth floor of the Robert Taylor Homes Projects. I had heard about the projects. Although I was brave enough to go to the South Side, venturing into the projects was another matter. Still, I had taken him up on his invitation, and I didn't want to make him feel like I was this arrogant White person, too good to go into his home. When we got upstairs, his wife was already asleep, as I suspected. We sat on the sofa and drank and talked. Somewhere between drinking and talking, I fell asleep and woke up to see the sun rising over Lake Michigan at six o'clock the next morning.

My wife, Jean wasn't too happy when I came home at seven. Unlike Clarence's wife, she had not gone to sleep, but rather stayed up all night worrying about me. That was one of the last times I witnessed a sunrise away from home.

Jean wasn't the only person concerned about me hanging out with "those people." My friends, co-workers, and even my Sears' managers had all become deeply troubled about the fact that I seemed to be throwing my life and certainly my career away by recklessly befriending Black people. They warned me that I was on the brink of losing my great job. "George, you have a good heart," they would say, "But these are not your people." They warned me of the dangers of venturing into Black neighborhoods.

I listened, not trying to explain myself because I knew I was once like them. Somewhere in the back of my mind were memories of times when I didn't just dislike Black people, I hated them. *But why?* I tried to reach back into the crevices of my memory and come up with the reasons I felt that way. The reasons were simple. Because hating Black people was the right thing to do. Because my mother and father were racists. Because my Uncle Lou was the most bigoted, racist person in town and to gain his favor and earn his love I had to learn racism and learn it well.

"Black neighborhoods are dangerous," my friends would tell me. Were they saying White neighborhoods are one hundred percent safe and all Black neighborhoods are one hundred percent unsafe?

"Are you saying Negroes are just as good as White people?" They would ask. Thoughts of Stepin Fetchit floated through my mind. If they were as good as us, what would be the purpose of those big Xs on the Sears' applications? "No," I would say, "That's not what I'm saying at all."

Working with the Prisoners and Ex-Prisoners through our Chicago Junior Chamber of Commerce Jaycees program, along with Father Charles "Dismas" Clark gave me a heart for inmates. I met a lot of ex-cons and found out many of them were decent people and life had somehow taken them in the wrong direction. One such person was Basil "the Owl" Banghart, who was part of the notorious "Purple Gang," headed up by Roger "The Terrible" Touhy. The Purple Gang was a real serious mob. Basil was one of the high-profile ex-convicts, but indeed a wonderful man. He had served twenty-seven years in federal prison, and by the time I met him, he was just returning to society.

Back then, the federal prisons were mainly for White people and the state and county jails predominately housed Black people. Father "Dismas" used to say, "If you're going to commit a crime, commit a federal crime. Then you go to clean, well-kept prisons."

Father "Dismas" and I tried to help Basil get placed on a job. Employers weren't enthusiastically seeking ex-convicts to place on their payrolls. Meanwhile, I had a house that seriously needed painting, so I hired Basil to do the job at half the rate a professional house painter would have charged. He did a fantastic job, and my wife, Jean, was very impressed. "Where did you get him?" she asked. I told her he was an ex-convict. She was pleased with the job, but not too pleased that I brought an ex-convict to our home. I wonder if Jean ever asked herself what she had gotten into, marrying a man who hangs out with Black people and brings ex-convicts to his home as handymen.

The more prisons I visited with Father "Dismas," the stronger my commitment to helping with the rehabilitation of prisoners and ex-prisoners grew. The convicts and ex-convicts loved Father "Dismas," and most importantly, they trusted him. Hollywood made a movie called the "The Hoodlum Priest," which was about Father "Dismas" and his work with convicts and ex-convicts.

One Christmas morning when I should have been home with my wife and children, I was riding with Father "Dismas," picking up celebrities and driving them to a penitentiary in Indiana to entertain the prisoners and help them celebrate Christmas. There was a Black comedian performing at that facility that day and he literally brought the house down. This guy was incredibly funny, but he wasn't a Stepin Fetchit or *Amos'n Andy* kind of funny. While their humor was designed to make people, especially White people, laugh at negative stereotypical portrayals of Black people; this comic entertained with an intelligent, thoughtful, logical kind of humor. His audience laughed with him rather than at him. After the performances, with pen and paper in hand, I looked for him to tell him how much I enjoyed his act and that I would like him to do a presentation for the Jaycees. There was so much going on that morning and so many people there; somehow he slipped out before I got a chance to say anything to him.

CHAPTER 10

Life Changing Friendships

"My best friend is the one who brings out the best in me."
–HENRY FORD

The more time I spent with "those people" the more comfortable I became being around them. Although I was successful at hiding my new associations from Jean and Uncle Lou, most of the sales staff at the Englewood store had somehow became aware of "George O'Hare's new friends," and the rumor mill was busy. This wasn't lost on my secretary, who stopped me a couple of months later as I was leaving the office.

"Mr. O'Hare," she said, "There is a Negro comedian performing at Mr. Kelly's, and I knew how much you liked—um—comedy, so I thought I'd tell you about it." She almost said she knew how much I liked "those people" Still, I was grateful for the information.

"I certainly do like comedy," I replied, "Do you know what time he's performing?"

She told me he would be performing all week, but my curiosity wouldn't allow me to wait another day. *A Negro comedian at Mr. Kelly's?* Mr. Kelly's was a nightclub on the Near North Side of Chicago and in those days, you never saw a single Black person in the place—not one. The waitresses were White, the bartender was White, the janitors were White, and the audience, of course, was lily-White. Once in a while, a Black musician like Duke Ellington or Cab Calloway would perform there, but a Black stand-up comedian? Never! I thought of *Amos 'n Andy,* and wondered if he was that kind of comedian. Since meeting Dr. King and the Black prison inmates in Father "Dismas'" program, I no longer found that type of comedy amusing. I began to understand why the NAACP had *Amos 'n Andy* taken off the air. No, I couldn't wait until the next day. I left work and headed straight for Mr. Kelly's.

When I arrived at the nightclub, I was greeted by the White doorman. As I walked into the smoke-filled room, all I saw was a sea of White faces at one table after another. The act hadn't started yet. Taking a table as close to the stage as possible, I ordered a drink and waited.

Finally, a White gentleman came up and took the microphone. After a brief moment of disappointment, I realized he wasn't the comic; he was only introducing the comic. "Put your hands together for the one and only Dick Gregory," he said. We politely applauded.

As soon as Dick Gregory took center stage, I recognized this slightly overweight, handsome comedian as the one who entertained the prisoners on Christmas morning of the previous year.

He smoked like a chimney—cigarette after cigarette- as he joked about racism so skillfully that it never occurred to this all-White audience that they were actually laughing at themselves and their racist ways.

"I went to a restaurant down south," he would say, "and the waitress told me, 'we don't serve Negroes,' and I said, 'that's okay, 'I don't eat Negroes, give me a half of a chicken."

Along with his hilarious jokes, he would also depict the not-so-funny reality of what our White ancestors did to other human beings during the slave era. As atrocious as these acts were, his jokes served to temper our shame and give us permission to laugh; not at the cruelty of our ancestors, but at the absurdity of their and our racist mindsets. Unlike a lot of stand-up comedians, Gregory was able to keep his audience in stitches without the use of profanity.

I couldn't wait to get to Sears the next day to thank my secretary for telling me about that show. When I left work that following evening, I again headed down to Mr. Kelly's. I wanted to see more of this guy. Maybe he'd repeat the same routine. I wouldn't have minded seeing it again, but I was pleasantly surprised when he told a whole new set of jokes.

The more I heard from Dick Gregory, the more I wanted to hear. I went back to Mr. Kelly's the following night and the next night and the night after that. On the fifth night, as I watched Dick Gregory bring his act to a close, I noticed he was looking directly at me. He told the audience how great they were, they applauded and he came straight to my table.

"You've been here every night." He said.

I nodded in agreement.

"Why do you keep coming back?" he asked

"Because I enjoy your jokes and you have new ones every night," I explained.

After the show he came and sat at my table and we talked until the waiters and bus boys began stacking the chairs on the tables.

"Which way are you going?" Gregory asked.

I told him I was going to the western suburbs. "Can I drop you off somewhere?" I volunteered.

He said he'd appreciate a ride to the L.

As we headed for the "L" station, I thought to myself, *Here I am, having a conversation with another intelligent Negro.* I had yet to meet one that matched Uncle Lou's description of a typical Negro. Surely there had to be more regular Negroes than there were exceptions, but at that time I had yet to encounter any typical head-scratching, shuffling, good-for-nothing Negroes.

Gregory wasn't just exceptional; he was brilliant. He knew something about everything under the sun. He called himself a "conspiracy theorist," but his theories made a lot of sense. He used to talk about putting on the "magic glasses." "George," he once told me, "If you ever put on the magic glasses you'll see through their propaganda and lies, and you'll never look at the world the same way again.

One night the conversation was so good I didn't want to stop when we got to the L, so I took him all the way home. He invited me to his beautifully decorated apartment, eloquently designed with white walls, black furniture, and black rugs. There was some irony in the fact that everything was black and white. I met his wife, Lillian, and his daughter, Michelle, the only child the Gregory's had at that time.

I cannot emphasize enough how Dick Gregory is the most intelligent, insightful, and genuine person I have ever known. Through those car rides, we developed a real friendship. Here was someone with whom I could be honest and truthful. I asked him so many questions about Negroes he began calling me his "racist friend." I didn't take offense because I knew he was right.

The experience of listening to the words of the Reverend Dr. Martin Luther King, Jr., and seeing up close his love for all people and his commitment to equality brought me close to becoming a "recovering racist." My friendship with Dick Gregory brought me even closer. I kept going to Mr. Kelly's or wherever Gregory was playing. Sometimes he'd tell his audience, "Honkies are dumb." They would laugh, and then he'd say. "If you don't believe it, look at that man sitting in the back. I call him a racist and he keeps coming back. Stand up "Honkie." That would be my cue. I'd stand up, and they'd laugh even harder.

He talked about the Constitution, too. "One of these days we're going to make this Constitution work," he'd say. "One day we're going to have a group of White executives talking about 'We have the best and the brightest working for us.' Then he'll look over at the door and say, 'Who's that Negro coming in here?' Another executive will say, 'Oh, that's my brother in law.'"

My friends, relatives, and coworkers weren't the only ones who were concerned about me hanging out in the Black community. I often wondered if Gordon Metcalf had known I would become so involved in the Black community would he have connected me with the Junior Chamber of Commerce or forced me to go see Dr. King speak? By that time, he had become Chairman of the Board of Sears, but I continued to have a good relationship with him.

One day he called me into his office and echoed what everyone else was saying.

"George, you're ruining your career," he said, "I know Dick Gregory is a nightclub comedian, but he's still a Negro, and I can't understand why you spend so much time with him.

I explained that Dick Gregory took an interest in me and opened my eyes to a whole new perspective of life. "I'd like to bring him down to meet you," I said.

Mr. Metcalf was open to meeting him, so I invited Dick Gregory to come to Sears. Now, usually, people couldn't get more than five minutes with the Chairman of the Board, but when I brought Dick Gregory to meet Mr. Metcalf that five-minute rule flew out of the window. In fact, Mr. Metcalf was so impressed with Gregory that he had all of the top management of Sears come to his office to meet him. Gregory spent more than an hour in Metcalf's office mesmerizing those managers with his profound logic and disarming humor.

When I told Gregory I knew Dr. King he said, "Good, maybe you'll learn something from him." He already knew Dr. King and knew he believed in the practice of "nonviolence" and "turning the other cheek." He also knew anyone who became part of Dr. King's movement had to commit to nonviolence, and Dick Gregory was becoming very much engaged in non-violent practices. Because of Gregory's anti-Vietnam war stance and his commitment to nonviolence, he even went on a serious fast, stopped eating meat and became a total vegetarian. He convinced me to stop eating meat, and I became a vegan also, for a little while. Eating meat was too deeply embroiled in my heritage to quit for good, but while I was a vegetarian, I went on a fast with Gregory and lost thirty pounds. I changed my bad eating habits a lot because of Greg. I'm not perfect, but I think I'm a healthier eater than a lot of people I know. Sometimes I joke that Gregory encouraged me to become a vegetarian, and at the same time, my love of beer caused me to become a "beer-a-tarian" all by myself.

When one thinks of a nonviolence movement, it generally conjures up visions of everyone peacefully walking, arm-in-arm, singing *Kumbaya*. That wasn't the case at all. The nonviolence movement was far from being quiet and peaceful as the name evoked. The marches and demonstrations elicited the worse kind of violence. The thought of how violence underscored the movement was running through my mind the day Dr. King scheduled a march in Marquette Park on the Southwest Side of Chicago. If he had asked me to go to the march, I would have had a hard time saying no, but deep down inside I was terrified at the thought of marching in that racist neighborhood with a group of Black people. Having once shared the racist mindset of my White brothers and sisters, I knew what would be in store for us. The Southwest Side residents would be out there protecting their all-White neighborhoods from those Negroes, just as we used to protect our all-White Chicago beaches from them. Some of the people who would be marching in Marquette Park that day could very well have been some of the White lifeguards from the Oak Street and North Avenue Beaches, all grown up and more embroiled in their racist views than ever. Whenever a Black person would come near our beach, we would shoo them off saying, "Go on Nigger! Get out of here!" The hatred that made us want to drown those Black people was the same type of ugly hatred that would cause the racists in Marquette Park to beat, stomp, stone or do whatever they felt was necessary to let the civil rights marchers know they're not welcome in their neighborhood.

I thought of my friends and neighbors calling me "Nigger lover," and warning me not to hang around "those people." Befriending a Black person was, in their racist minds, equivalent to an act of treason. Although I understood the necessity of the marches and agreed in principle, I was not prepared to go out there and put my life on the line. I had a wife, I had three sons, and I had a life. Martin must have read my mind.

"George," he said, "There will probably be a lot of calls coming in, especially from the press. Why don't you stay here at the church and answer the phones?"

"I'll be happy to," I said. I didn't know if he could detect the relief in my voice. Knowing Martin, he probably could.

Later, when I was at home, and Jean and I were watching the march on TV, I watched, horrified as Dr. King was hit with a brick causing him to fall to one knee. I thought to myself, *if it hadn't been for Dr. King, I might have been the recipient of that brick or something worse.*

There were thirty injuries in all that March afternoon, but that didn't stop Dr. King. He planned another march in Birmingham, Alabama. Dick Gregory went with him, but Dr. King thought it would be best if I stayed in Chicago. Once again, I couldn't have agreed more. The next evening, I got a call from Dick Gregory.

"Hey George, I'm here in Birmingham."

"Oh, you're still there?"

"Yeah, they arrested Dr. King and me, along with some other marchers."

"Did they let you go?"

"Yeah, they let us all go … to jail."

"You've been arrested?"

"That's what I said! We're in the Birmingham Jail. Do you think you can let the newspapers know?"

"I'll do my best," I told him.

Since I was the advertising manager for Sears, I knew a lot of media people. They knew I was the one who made the decisions about what ad space to buy for Sears' advertising, so they were more than accommodating when I wanted to give them a 'scoop' for their papers. Some of the media people became more than reporters to me; we became friends. Irv Kupcinet, the legendary columnist for the *Chicago Sun-Times* newspaper, became one of my closest friends. His "Kup's Column" was the most widely read and frequently quoted column of any Chicago newspaper. As soon as I finished talking to Dick Gregory, I began dialing Irv Kupcinet's number. "Hey Kup," I said, "I've got an exclusive for you." Kup was all ears, and I didn't disappoint.

"Dr. Martin Luther King and Dick Gregory are in a Birmingham jail," I told him. Kup wanted all of the details. I did my best to paint a picture for him, based on what Gregory told me.

The next day I bought a *Chicago Sun-Times* newspaper and turned to Kup's Column. There was the story, "Dr. Martin Luther King and Dick Gregory were arrested and are in a Birmingham, Alabama jail." The other newspapers, the *Chicago Daily News*, the *Herald American* and the *Chicago Tribune*, as well as some smaller newspapers, picked up the story. The *Sun-Times* sent a photographer to Alabama to take a photo of Gregory and Dr. King behind bars. After that, "Kup" became very interested in the Civil Rights Movement. Nearly every day there was a mention of Dr. King or Dick Gregory in "Kup's Column."

Gregory remained a guest of the Birmingham jail for four days. Why this successful comedian would decide to go to Birmingham, knowing his arrest was inevitable, was a mystery to most people, and Gregory knew it He made a speech at St. John's Baptist Church to explain why he made the decision, and newspapers across the country quoted him. The Civil Rights Movement became a prominent daily item in the national news, and Dick Gregory was officially a part of that movement.

Membership in most organizations has its privileges. Membership in the controversial Civil Rights Movement had its pitfalls, and for Gregory, that meant immediately losing over 150 nightclub engagements at an average of $20,000 per event. In a matter of days, Gregory went from a sought-after comedian with a multi-million dollar career to being almost on the edge of poverty.

Losing such income didn't seem to bother Gregory. He was on a mission to bring an end to Jim Crow, racism, the Vietnam War, and worldwide hunger. My personal commitment to the Civil Rights Movement was becoming stronger each day and it was keeping me away from home almost every night. Those thoughts were going through my head on one particular night when I was at a Civil Rights rally. Dr. King interrupted my thoughts;

"George, my work is taking me away from Chicago for the next several months," he said.

I quietly breathed a sigh of relief. While I had grown very fond of Dr. King and would miss seeing him, I felt that his being out of the city would give me a chance to spend more time with my family.

"I understand, Dr. King," I told him, "And if you ever need me for anything just let me know."

Dr. King smiled and said, "I'd like you to meet somebody."

I followed him to the other side of the room where a tall, handsome twenty-three-year-old young man, wearing a tee-shirt, dungarees, and gym shoes was talking to a small group. Others stood around waiting their turn. Dr. King took me to the front of the line and introduced me to the young man.

"This is Jesse Jackson," he said, "I want you to volunteer and do for him what you have been doing for me."

What I had been doing for Dr. King was getting publicity and news coverage for the events and marches he led, keeping the public informed of his speaking engagements and accompanying him to meetings and events. Although my looking forward to a much-needed break from that hectic schedule was short-lived, I was confident that Jesse Jackson's needs would be nowhere near as demanding as Rev. King's were. I shook Jesse's hand and told him I would be pleased to volunteer for him.

At the end of the meeting, Jesse Jackson found me.

"Dr. King told me you worked for Sears, Roebuck and Company," he said. Dr. King always included that fact whenever he introduced me to someone, as if working for Sears was a prestigious accomplishment.

"That's right," I replied.

Then Jesse said, "Can you get me a discount on an air conditioner?"

He explained he lived in an attic apartment with only one window and his wife was pregnant. I told him I would look around for an air conditioner that was returned and Sears would probably give him a good deal on it.

"Come down to my office in the morning," I said.

"What time?" he asked.

"Just get there early," I told him.

Even though my workday didn't begin until nine a.m., I always arrived at Sears no later than seven o'clock in the morning. As I approached the store, I was mentally making plans for the morning. First I would get my coffee, then read the paper, maybe make a couple of phone calls—I told Jesse Jackson to get there early, but I figured early for him would be around 10 am. Although Black people were wonderful human beings, based on what Uncle Lou had told me all of my life, I knew being on time was not one of their strong points.

The security guard at the Sears employee entrance greeted me saying, "Mr. O'Hare, there's a fellow in your office waiting for you—he's been here about an hour." Sure enough, when I got to my office, young Jesse Jackson was sitting there, patiently waiting for me. *So much for reading the paper.*

I offered him some coffee, and we began to talk about the problems of the world as we waited for the store to open. As he went on about his world view, his perspective on what was going on in the political scene, and his predictions for the future, it occurred to me that I was in the company of a twenty-three-year-old genius. For one so young to be so passionate about uplifting the Black race and helping to level the playing field was impressive, to say the least. If I hadn't been sitting there, facing him, I wouldn't have believed that all of this wisdom could come out of the mind and the mouth of a young man only a few years out of his teens. We talked for over two and a half hours. I understood what Dr. King saw in this great young man.

When the store opened at nine a.m. I took Jesse down to the sales floor to introduce him to the employees. He didn't just say, "Hello, how are you?" He engaged everyone he met in a conversation. "What do you do? How long have you been here?" It was evident that he wasn't just making small talk; he was genuinely interested in their answers.

We went to the Large Appliances Department, and I asked the salesman to help Jesse find an air conditioner at a good price. Jesse picked out an Air Conditioner, a TV set, and some other discounted appliances. He explained that Civil Rights was a non-profit profession that didn't command large salaries. With his incredible mind, I figured that he could be making well over six figures if he was in the private sector. On second thought, being Black, he probably wouldn't get much of a salary no matter how smart he was—even in the private sector.

When I went back upstairs to my office, my phone was ringing. It was one of my co-workers. "Who was that guy?" he asked. The phones kept ringing most of the morning. "Is he coming back?" "Where'd you meet him?" My co-workers were impressed and seemed surprised to meet such a wonderfully intelligent and charismatic young man who happened to be Black.

Later that evening, Jesse and I met and talked about the kind of work I would be doing for him. It was a lot more than I expected. We developed a great relationship and for six and a half years I volunteered for him around the clock. It was clear that he understood how valuable the media was in terms of getting his message to the public. Keeping him in the news was relatively easy for me since, as an advertising buyer for Sears I knew most of the columnists, reporters and editorial staff.

Dr. King founded an organization called the Southern Christian Leadership Conference (SCLC). The economic arm of SCLC was Operation Breadbasket, and Dr. King designated Jesse Jackson as its leader. Volunteering for Jesse Jackson meant being at all of the Operation Breadbasket meetings. I was faithfully in attendance, every Saturday morning. Later, Jesse renamed Operation Breadbasket, Operation PUSH (People United to Serve Humanity).

Around the time that I had begun volunteering for Jesse Jackson, the Chicago street gangs were gaining prominence. Jesse knew all of the gang leaders and most of the members. On one occasion he held a forum at PUSH and invited the gangs. About five hundred of them showed up, including the dynamic Jeff Fort. Jeff was the leader of the Blackstone Rangers, which later became the El Rukins. Larry Hoover, who headed the Black Disciples, was also there. Both of these young men had excellent leadership abilities, and I believe that if they had chosen another direction, they would have surely been outstanding.

One of the speakers at PUSH that afternoon was a young Black man by the name of John Davis. John was a news anchor for Channel Five, *NBC-TV*. As I listened to him speak, I thought, *Here is another exceptional Black person.* I was beginning to think; *maybe Black people weren't inherently dumb, slow, lazy, and happy-go-lucky. Maybe they weren't all trifling as my Uncle Lou said.* So far, I hadn't met one, not one Black person who acted like Stepin Fetchit or *Amos 'n Andy*.

John Davis' speech was very impressive, the gang leaders listened attentively,applauding every once in awhile. They were very respectful and not a single one of them kept his hat on in the auditorium. Having been raised to believe all Black people were criminals, once again I had to rethink my racist beliefs.

"The media decides the way it reports the news to make people think the worst about Black people," John Davis explained, "You see, when a Black man kills a Black man, you're instructed to show the Black perpetrator. When a Black man kills a White man, you show the Black perpetrator and the White victim. When a White man kills a Black man, you show the Black victim. And when a White man kills a White man, you don't show the perpetrator; you only show the White victim."

Davis also spoke about how the editor decides the focus of the news, the angles, what stories make the news and which ones end up on the cutting room floor. "That's why if you turn to Channel 2, 5 or 7, you're going to see the same stories and the same footage, and it almost always makes Whites look good, and Blacks look bad." My mind quickly flashed back to images of a crime scene where reporters interviewed Black women with rags tied around their head, or Black men who couldn't talk very well. It was as if those journalists would find the worse looking people on the block to put before the cameras. Now I understood that it was planned that way in many instances, and that the media was complicit in creating the images that helped promote our racist mindsets.

Reverend Jackson gave the closing speech, and it was powerful. The theme of the meeting was "self-help" and "self-determination," and Jesse spoke of how after slavery, Black people were taught to be consumers but not manufacturers. He said that meant that Black people would always be dependent on Whites for their products and services and even their jobs.

On most evenings I would leave Sears heading for PUSH instead of heading home. Reverend Jesse Jackson never stopped working or thinking of new things to do. One evening he asked me if I could come to the PUSH headquarters the next morning.

"Well, I have to go to work in the morning," I explained.

"What time do you have to be there?"

"Nine o'clock,"

"Maybe you could come before you go to work,"

"Sure! What time?"

"Oh, about two thirty."

"In the MORNING??"

I didn't dare set the alarm, because I didn't want to wake up my wife, Jean. So I slept until about one forty-five in the morning, then forced myself out of bed, took a shower, and dressed. I was about to creep out of the house when Jean called out.

"George, where are you going at this time of morning?"

"Jesse wants me to come to PUSH," I said, "We're planning another session with the gang leaders."

"Gang leaders?" she repeated.

Try as I may, I could never convince Jean that the gang leaders were decent people.

"One day I'm going to bring them by here to meet you." I told her.

"I don't want to meet them," she said.

A couple of weeks later, I told Jean I wanted to have some friends over for drinks. She was all for the idea. At least that would keep me at home instead of out somewhere marching with those Black people. I invited Jeff Fort, Larry Hoover and five other gang leaders to the house. We had a splendid time, just talking about everything under the sun. Surprisingly, my wife was enjoying them as much as I was.

When they left, my wife said, "Those were nice young men. Where did you meet them?"

"Those are the gang leaders of Chicago," I said.

She stared at me intently to make sure I wasn't joking. "You brought gang leaders to our house?" She said. But her next words were a surprise. "They're very nice."

Once again that song came to my mind, *To know them is to love them.* You really can't know people based on what others say about them—but once you get to know them for yourself, then you learn to love them. If I had told my wife I was going to bring seven gang members to the house, she would have said "No way." But I brought seven gang members, and she could only say "They're very nice."

Volunteering for PUSH brought me in contact with a lot of wonderful people, like the very Reverend Willie Taplin Barrow. This little woman with a big spirit and a magnificent presence became a very close friend. It was Reverend Barrow who labeled me a "recovering racist," but she meant it in a positive way.

After the March on Washington, I began marching with Dr. King, Jesse Jackson, and others. Reverend Barrow and I would always be together, arm-in-arm.

Reverend Jesse Jackson also introduced me to a beautiful, smart, and wonderful young woman by the name of Hermene Hartman. Hermene and I became such good friends that some people accused us of "going together." I assured them that I was very much in love with my wife and my friendship with Hermene was purely platonic. Sometimes she'd invite me to lunch or dinner at her house. I met her mother and her father, Herman, who she was named after. When I think of the women of the Civil Rights Movement, Hermene Hartman, Reverend Willie Barrow, Mrs. Jacqueline Jackson and the great Reverend Jessie "Ma" Houston—I think of how important they were to the movement, and also how important they were in my becoming a recovering racist. Each of them, in their own way, took me under their "Angel wings" and helped me to become very comfortable as a member of PUSH.

My White friends and neighbors and even strangers and local media could not understand the dedication of this White, Irish Catholic to a movement led by a Black, Baptist preacher. When they'd get me alone, they'd question me.

"George, why do you spend more time with Negroes than you do with the White community?" someone asked. "How can you be so involved in this Civil Rights Movement, and you're a Catholic?"

"What does my being a Catholic have to do with my being in the Civil Rights Movement?" I'd ask.

"You're always hanging out with Baptist Ministers; you should be hanging out with Catholic Priests."

"But the Civil Rights Movement is about Black people," was my response, All of the Catholic Priests are White. There are no Black Catholic Priests."

From across the room, someone said, "Yes, there are Black Catholic Priests. At least I know of one."

I looked around to see who said that. It was my friend John Calloway. John was a committed Civil Rights advocate long before he and I developed a friendship. He knew the Movement and all the players from top to bottom and had once produced a 13-segment, award-winning documentary about segregation called, "*The House Divided.*" *He may know a lot about Civil Rights*, I thought, *but he doesn't know the Catholic church. They punished a nun for giving little White children a card with a Black man's face on it. They wouldn't even allow a little Black boy to spend more than a day in one of their classrooms. How then,* I wondered, *would these same racist Catholics allow a Black man to be a priest?*

"No, there are no Black Catholic Priests," I said. "Not one, I'm sure."

But John was insistent.

"Yes, there is a Black Catholic Priest," he repeated.

"I've never heard of a Black Catholic Priest in my entire life," I argued.

"Then you've never heard of Father George Clements, the Black Catholic Priest at St. Dorothy's Parish."

I still couldn't believe it. "Where is St. Dorothy's?" I asked.

He told me the church was on the South Side of Chicago. I took down the address. "There are only two kinds of people in the world;" Uncle Lou would always say. "White, Irish Catholics and those that wished they were White, Irish Catholics." *So, how does a Black Catholic priest fit into this world?* I asked myself.

John knew me well enough to know that I wouldn't stop until my curiosity had been satisfied.

"So, let me guess," He said, "Tomorrow you will leave Sears and head right over to St. Dorothy's Church."

"Tomorrow?" I said, "Tomorrow is too far away." I was already putting on my coat and hat. "I'm going there right now."

St. Dorothy's was a big, beautiful structure; as most Catholic churches are. There were four separate buildings—the church, the school, the rectory and the convent—but they were all connected and took up nearly a full city block. I walked up the stairs of the rectory, which was on the Vernon Avenue side of the church, and rang the bell. A pleasant, African American woman answered the door, and I explained that I had come to see Father George Clements. Still not believing a Black Catholic Priest existed, I halfway expected her to say, "Oh, there's no Father Clements; that's just a myth someone made up about a Black priest." Then we'd have a good laugh. "He's in a meeting," she said, "But if you don't mind waiting . . ." "I don't mind," I said.

The housekeeper led me to a small room in the Rectory. "Father will probably be meeting for at least an hour," she said. "I'll wait," I repeated.

Less than ten minutes had passed when a tall, handsome, freckled-face Black man, wearing full clergy garb with a White collar came into the room. John was right. He was a Black priest alright. I could barely believe my eyes. "Are you looking for me?" he asked. "Yes, Father," I said, "I'm George O'Hare, and I volunteer in the Civil Rights Movement. I heard there was a Black Catholic Priest here, so I came to meet you." Father Clements smiled. "Oh, I'm not the only Black Catholic Priest," he said. Then he took me upstairs to a room where he had been meeting with seven other Black priests. I was amazed.

Father Clements explained they had been trying to get Cardinal Cody to recognize the Black priests in the Archdiocese. "Maybe I can help," I volunteered, and explained that I was already volunteering to do public relations for Dr. King and Jesse Jackson. My plan to help them gain recognition was met with great enthusiasm. I couldn't let them down.

Cardinal Cody was stubborn, but I was determined, and I had no intention of giving up. I didn't mind telling Cardinal Cody how racists I felt the Catholic Church was. He vehemently denied being racist, but I believe he knew I was right and gradually he began to soften a little – just a little. I was relentless, and finally, Cardinal Cody agreed to recognize Black priests as being a part of the Archdiocese. That's one of the accomplishments in my life I really appreciate because I could have left the Catholic Church if he had not agreed to be receptive to the Black priests in the Archdiocese.

About that time, the Pastor of St. Dorothy's, Father Scanlan, was stepping down. With an eighty percent Black congregation and a predominately Black student body, Father Scanlan reasoned that a Black priest, namely Father Clements, should be the Pastor. Everyone agreed. Well, almost everyone. Cardinal Cody barely wanted Black priests in the denomination; he certainly did not want any one of them to pastor one of Chicago's churches. Finally, after much persuasion from the Black community, Cardinal Cody named a Black priest as pastor, but it wasn't Father Clements. Father Roland Lambert was imported from another parish to shepherd St. Dorothy's Congregation. What a slap in the face to Father Clements who was already at St. Dorothy's, and was loved by the entire congregation.

Father Clements and I became friends almost immediately, so I took this disappointment very personally. I knew that Cardinal Cody probably thought to appoint any Black priest was satisfactory. He was wrong, and something had to be done to show him just how wrong he was.

The press had been instrumental in helping to get recognition for the Black priests, and they helped put pressure on Cardinal Cody to at least appoint a Black priest, even if it wasn't the right one as far as we were concerned. So I went to my friend Irv Kupcinet, and Kup ran the story in the *Chicago Sun-Times*.

The article was like a battle cry for many Chicagoans who came out in droves to peacefully protest the Cardinal's decision. Father Lambert was well-liked, so it is important to note that the marches were not to protest his appointment, but rather to protest the Cardinal purposely overlooking Chicago's beloved

Father Clements. The protests continued until Cardinal Cody succumbed to the pressure and finally made Father Clements Pastor over Holy Angels Catholic Church on Oakenwald Boulevard in Chicago's Bronzeville community.

Compared to the beautiful St. Dorothy's Church and school in Chicago's middle-class Chatham neighborhood, Holy Angels seemed like a slum. Attendance was down. It was one of the oldest, but poorest churches in the community. However, Father Clements turned that church around. He created a music and drama program called "The Little Angels," which showcased the immense talent of select Holy Angels students. People throughout Chicago learned of the excellent curriculum and began enrolling their children into Holy Angels. After a couple of years of Father Clements' pastoring Holy Angels, people from all over Chicago, not just Holy Angels' immediate community, began sending their children to Holy Angels Catholic School. Soon it became one of the most sought after schools in Chicago, and a waiting list was established to accommodate the escalating enrollment. The Rectory at Holy Angels became like my second home since I was there so often.

If someone had told me twenty years prior that a Black person could go to seminary and become a priest; I would have said "No way!" But I was finally beginning to see that Dr. King, Jesse Jackson, Dick Gregory, Hermene Hartman, Reverend Barrow, John Davis and now, Father Clements were not exceptions to the Black community; they were representatives of the Black community I never knew existed.

I continued to watch my friend, Dick Gregory, evolve from a comedian to a Civil Rights advocate, a human rights advocate and a health care guru. When Gregory committed himself to a cause, he was in for the long haul in every sense. He didn't just protest the Viet Nam War; he committed to prayer and fasting for the war to end.

Gregory and I shared a love for sports. He loved running and had been a champion track star in his high school days. During my high school and college years, I was a champion swimmer. He ran in the Army; I swam in the Navy.

Gregory continued to run as he advocated ending world hunger. Besides fasting for long periods of time, he also ran nine hundred miles, from Chicago to Washington, D.C. A couple of years later, he jogged from Los Angeles to

New York. Gregory was serious about his commitment to the health of America as well as the world. I witnessed him study the human body for nine years, after which he created an incredible energy-giving product that he called the 4X Formula. Gregory took the 4X Formula for energy and nourishment when running cross-country. Pretty soon, he began to help others with that incredible Formula. Gregory sent three tons of the Formula to an Ethiopian hospital during a severe drought and saved thousands of children from starving. He helped celebrities, like Michael Jackson's brother, Randy Jackson. Randy was in a terrible automobile accident and might have lost his legs if it had not been for Gregory and his 4X Formula. The Pittsburg Pirates baseball team praised Dick Gregory and his product for giving their team the energy to become world champions.

Gregory shocked the world when he flew 300 tons of food to the starving White Appalachians. The Junior Chamber of Commerce, just like practically everything else in the nation, was segregated. That changed when Dick Gregory became the first Black member of the Jaycees.

As busy as I was doing my job for Sears and being active in the Jaycees, I still managed to spend a good deal of time as a de facto public relations person for Jesse Jackson, just as I had volunteered to conduct public relations for Dr. King. Anytime the making of a news story presented itself, whether it was about Dr. King, Jesse Jackson or the Civil Rights Movement in general, I would find myself surrounded by reporters with their microphones in my face asking for a statement. When a story appeared the following day, it would read, "George O'Hare, volunteer Public Relations representative for Dr. King or Reverend Jackson, gave the following statement." *Well, Uncle Lou*, I would think to myself, *what do you think of your little racist nephew growing up to be a spokesman for the Black community?*

CHAPTER 11

Discovering Soul Music

"Music is the highway that crosses over obstacles and brings people together.
It's the bridge over troubled waters."
–GEORGE O'HARE.

Throughout my career at Sears, I sold every product at one time or another. But a significant turning point in my life occurred when I began to sell phonograph records and became the advertising manager of Sears. It marked an important milestone on my road to recovery from the "mortal sin of racism" that stigmatized my early life.

As merchandising manager over Sears' big and small appliances, I was also the promotional manager for the TV and High Fidelity Phonograph Department, which included all 45-RPM records and record albums. Dick Gregory and I spoke every day, and on one occasion he told me he had visited the TV and HiFi Department at Sears Englewood store. At that time, the Englewood store at 63rd

and Halsted Street was rapidly changing; there were fewer White customers and a great deal more Black customers.

"Did you see our big display?" I asked proudly.

"I saw Elvis Presley records and his image on some big posters."

"That's our display! Elvis Presley, his albums and 45-RPM records are going to be our best sellers!

"George," Gregory said; "Black people don't want to hear Elvis Presley. If you put Sam Cooke's records in the store and then advertise them, your customers will line up to buy every one of his recordings!"

Although I had never heard of Sam Cooke, I valued Dick Gregory's advice. "Where can I get Sam Cooke's records?" I asked. "Here, take this number," Gregory said. It was the phone number of Ernie Leaner who was a top Black record distributor and also the brother of Al Benson, the great Black radio disc jockey. Al Benson was the first Black person to have his own radio music show. When I called Ernie Leaner and told him I needed Sam Cooke's records for Sears, he immediately accommodated me by having all of Cooke's newest 45's and albums delivered to all of the Chicago Sears stores. Gregory's advice was right. As soon as we put those records on display and put posters up in our stores showing Sam Cooke and featuring his records, Sears' record sales shot up overnight.

After that, records and albums of all the top Black Entertainment artists, like Al Green, the Temptations, Aretha Franklin, Isaac Hayes and of course, Sam Cooke, could be found at all Sears stores. Records and albums became the top sales and profit item in all of our 45-plus Midwest Sears stores in Chicago and throughout Illinois.

Ads promoting the records and albums appeared in all the newspapers, including the *Chicago Sun-Times*, the *Chicago Tribune*, the *Chicago Daily News,* and the *Herald American*. We were doing great, or so I thought. One day Gregory asked me, "Why are you advertising to Black people in the White papers?" I was puzzled. "What other newspapers are there?" Gregory smiled and shook his head like he always did to express his amazement at how clueless I was about the Black community. Then he began to introduce me to the Black community newspapers and the largest Black newspaper in Chicago, the *Chicago Defender*. As soon as I began placing advertising in the Black newspapers, customers began coming into the store in droves, asking for the records featured in our newspaper ads.

"Business can't get any better than this," I bragged to Gregory one day.

"Yes, it can," he said, "Why are you only advertising in newspapers?"

"Because when people go through the paper looking for sales, they'll see what we have in the record department and they may come in to buy some of our 45-RPM records or even some record albums," I explained.

But Gregory had an entirely different viewpoint. "There's a big difference between reading the artist's name and the title of their recording and actually hearing the music. When people hear just a little bit of a recording, they'll start nodding their heads and patting their feet and they'll want to hear more," he explained, "so if you play a little bit of the music and tell them the record is available at Sears, they'll come to Sears to buy it."

The only radio programs I was familiar with, besides dramas like *The Shadow Knows* or comedies like *Fibber McGee and Molly*, was *Walter Winchell* or *Don McNeill's Breakfast Club*, and I couldn't imagine playing Black music on any of those shows. Gregory explained that just like there were Black newspapers, there were also Black radio stations, which featured Black deejays that played Black music.

After we started advertising on the radio, record sales in our Chicagoland stores went from $3 million to $35 million in one year. Gregory was right again.

We spent a lot of money on Black radio, and the radio stations and disc jockeys loved Sears, Roebuck and Company. Gregory introduced me to the Chicago Disc Jockey, Holmes Daylie, who everyone called "Daddy-O" Daylie, as well as Sid McCoy, Herb Kent, Sam Cook and "Butterball."

Daddy-O Daylie was famous for his charismatic style. He was a smooth talker who had a way with words and in that respect, he reminded me of my Uncle "Husk." Just like people tuned into Uncle "Husk's" broadcast, people throughout the community would stop whatever they were doing and tune in to the Daddy-O Daylie show which he always started off in the same way, "This is your musical host who loves you most." He even had a colorful way of breaking for the news: "And now, old Midnight Sun, don't run before we pay our musical dues. We want to take you on a five-minute cruise through the world's latest news."

I would go to the studio to find out what the newest records were so we could put them on display. Sometimes Daddy-O would stop by Sears to pick up a check for advertising. I was still learning about the Black community, and Daddy-O seemed to get a kick out of answering my questions.

One day I was telling him about a Black person's home where I had demonstrated a vacuum cleaner. That homeowner had top-of-the-line everything: Persian rugs, custom drapes, and mahogany furnishings

"Why do Black people buy the most expensive furniture, the most expensive cars, the most expensive everything?" I asked him.

"Well, George," 'Daddy-O' laughed, "We can't buy a home in your neighborhood, so we buy the best of everything for the inside of our homes in our neighborhoods. And even though we can't live in your White neighborhoods, we can drive through them in our brand new Cadillac cars."

In the summer of 1963, Dr. King and some other Civil Rights Leaders decided to organize a March on Washington for jobs and freedom. Everybody in the Movement, involved in the Movement or who knew anything about the Movement knew about that March and planned to be in attendance. There were buses leaving out of every city. Some people were taking trains or carpooling. Those who could afford airfare were making plans to fly to Washington. "Daddy-O" Daylie offered to pay my airfare, hotel, and other expenses so I could be there with him.

"This is history, George," he said, "You don't want to miss this."

I thought about it and thought about it. *What if the crowd becomes hostile?* I wondered. *What if protesters are there harassing the marchers?* There were many people in the White communities and even some in the Black community who didn't like Dr. King. During the Civil Rights era, they thought he was a troublemaker. One group of Black preachers said they were the victims of Black and White hostility because of Dr. King and they pulled out their guns and said to him, "Quit this marching and protesting at our churches and get out of Chicago." *Would those preachers come to Washington and fire their guns in protest?*

Then I had another thought: *What if they televised the March? What if I went to the March and some of my White friends or co-workers saw me on TV marching with Dr. King and the other Black people? If Uncle Lou saw me on national television sitting next to a "nigger preacher," I'd never hear the end of it. And what would my wife, Jean say?* Daddy-O was right, the March on Washington for Jobs and Freedom was an event I didn't want to miss. But once again that fear of being a lone White man in a crowd of Black people and being called "nigger-lover" took hold of my brain and wouldn't let go. "No, I've got too much work at Sears to do; I just can't afford to take off," I told Daddy-O.

As it turned out, I did take the day off. Even though I was afraid to go to the March, I still wanted to see it in its entirety, and there was no way I could sit around watching a group of Black people marching, while I was supposed to be working.

My family wasn't too interested in watching the March, so I told Jean since I was off I'd paint the kitchen. I didn't get very much painting done that day. I sat glued to the television, watching the march. The "group of Black people" I had envisioned turned out to be over 200,000 men, women, and a few children and there seemed to be just as many White people among the marchers as there were Black. As I watched Jesse Jackson, his beautiful wife Jacqueline,and so many of my friends marching arm-in-arm and singing "We Shall Overcome, " I began to regret that I had turned down "Daddy-O" Daylie's offer.

When the marchers reached the Lincoln Memorial, the Program began. First, there were musical performances by Marian Anderson, Joan Baez, Bob Dylan, Mahalia Jackson, Peter, Paul and Mary and Josh White. After the musical entertainment, the speeches began. The actor, Charlton Heston, read a speech which was supposed to have been written by James Baldwin. Later, someone said that the speech was written for James Baldwin, but he refused to read it, which is why Charlton Heston ended up reading it.

As I listened to speaker after speaker deliver poignant, moving messages, I felt a terrible knot in my stomach. Why, oh, why didn't I go to the March with "Daddy-O"? I could have been marching arm-in-arm with my friends of the Movement, instead of standing in the kitchen with a bucket of paint watching and wishing I was there. John Lewis, representing the Student Nonviolent

Coordinating Committee gave a moving speech. But when my friend, Dr. Martin Luther King, Jr., came to the podium, I began to cry. With tears streaming down my face, I listened to him talk about his dream of a nation where people were judged, not by the color of their skin, but the content of their character. The speech was moving, but that's not why I was crying. My tears were tears of regret that by not taking the opportunity that Daddy-O offered to me, I missed attending that once-in-a-lifetime event.

When Gregory returned from Washington, I told him how badly I felt about not going.

"That was my chance to be a part of history," I moaned.

"You are a part of History," Gregory said, "You know more well-known Negroes than the average Negro knows."

He was right. Besides the Civil Rights leaders and people in the movement, somebody's manager was also calling me nearly every day to see if their artist could come and sign autographs to boost their phonograph record sales at the local Sears stores.

Between my position as advertising manager at Sears and my friendship with Dick Gregory, I met plenty of celebrities. It was nothing for Isaac Hayes, Sam Cooke, Billy Eckstein or Ramsey Lewis to stop by the store to promote a recent record or album. All of the entertainers that I became acquainted with were not Black. I met Frank Sinatra, and the great singer, Tony Bennett even took my wife and me out for dinner and drinks once. Needless to say, Jean was thrilled.

One day my secretary buzzed me and said, "Mr. O'Hare, there's someone on the phone who says he represents a comedian named Bill Cosby. He wants to schedule an autograph signing." "Get a number and tell him I'll call back," I said. I had scheduled plenty of autograph signings for singers and musicians, but a comedian? I dialed Dick Gregory.

"Greg, there's a comedian named Bill Cosby who wants to have an autograph signing at Sears,"

"Well, what's the problem? Let him come." Greg said.

"But you're the only real comedian," I said. "I don't want to support anyone who would in any way compete with you."

Gregory said, "Listen. This guy Cosby is super, and he has a different kind of comedy. White folks love him because he tells jokes about Negroes and Negro family life."

I was still reluctant, but I said "Okay."

"And don't advertise Cosby on the Negro radio stations," Gregory warned. "Negroes are not going to come to see him. Ask your boss for a bigger advertising budget to promote his appearance on White stations."

We scheduled autograph signings for Cosby at four stores in the Negro neighborhoods, including the Sears Englewood store. "You're not sending him to any White stores?" Gregory said incredulously. I told him my bosses wouldn't look on me favorably if I wasted their money sending a Negro to a Sears store in an all-White neighborhood. Nevertheless, just because Gregory suggested it, I scheduled him at the Sears store in the all-White community of Irving Park and Cicero. About a handful of Black people came to the autograph signings at the stores in the Black areas—79th Street, 63rd and Western, and the Englewood stores. But when the announcement came that Bill Cosby would be at the White neighborhood store at Irving Park and Cicero Avenue, much to our surprise, so many people showed up we had to hire Andy Frain ushers and ask the Chicago police to help us with crowd control.

Cosby told a few jokes, and the crowd liked him a lot. He was funny, but in my opinion, he wasn't nearly as entertaining or as informative as Dick Gregory.

After the event, Cosby took me to dinner at Jimmy Wong's Chinese Restaurant in downtown Chicago. I thought he wanted to talk about his records, but as soon as we sat down, he began talking about his brother, Russell.

"Russell needs a job," he told me.

"Okay," I said, "I'll see what I can do."

"He lives in Philadelphia," Cosby said.

"Not a problem. We have Sears's stores in Philadelphia. I'll make a phone call."

"Listen," said Cosby very earnestly, "Don't put him in any kind of management training program. Give him a job in the warehouse sweeping floors."

The next day, Cosby left for Japan to begin shooting the *I Spy* Television series. I phoned the Philadelphia office and gave them Russell's information.

The manager I spoke with said he'd take care of everything. Sears hired Russell immediately. A few days later, Bill Cosby was on the phone angrily screaming at the top of his voice.

"I told you to get my brother, Russell a job sweeping floors!"

"Isn't that what they did?"

"They put him in a store management training program! He came home and told my mother, and she called me!" Cosby was furious.

The next day I called the manager at the Sears store in Philadelphia and explained the situation. They switched Russell to the warehouse, sweeping floors. Russell was happy, Cosby was happy, and I was very relieved.

Russell Cosby was very lucky that I was able to meet with his brother, Bill, at Jimmy Wongs. Any other night, I would have been at a meeting. After the March on Washington, an evening didn't go by when there wasn't some type of meeting organized by one of the civil rights groups. Every night I would leave Sears and head to the home of Dr. Odom, the dentist, or the home of George Jones, Vice President of the Joe Louis Milk Company, or the Chicago Urban League, or one of the churches. Sometimes the meetings would go on past midnight.

One thing I learned about the people in the movement; they loved to talk. There was no such thing as a short meeting in the Black community, because every comment turned into a speech. On one particular evening, the meeting I was attending seemed to go on and on, but I was enjoying the speeches. When I heard my name called, I looked around and saw George Jones motioning for me to come to the side of the room where he was standing. "Listen," he said, "This meeting is going to go on for a long time, and Dr. King is supposed to have an interview with Wesley South on his radio show, "Hotline." Do you think you can drive him to the WVON Radio Studio?" I didn't mind at all. I relished the times when I was alone with Dr. King. We always talked about everything in the world of race relations and civil rights, and I learned something from each of those conversations.

Wesley South's "Hotline" was the only radio show in Chicago that interviewed Negroes. The word had gotten out that Dr. King was going to be there. When we pulled into the parking lot, it was full of people who wanted to greet him, say hello, shake his hand, and tell him what a great thing he was doing for the

Negro community. When we finally made our way through the crowd into the studio, Wesley South, and his assistants grabbed Dr. King and pulled him into the studio.

There I was in the studio's lobby by myself. At least I thought I was by myself. I picked up one of the magazines off a table in the foyer and began thumbing through it. Suddenly I got an eerie feeling that I was being watched. "Stared at" would be a more accurate description. I turned around and saw this young, tall, handsome Black man with the biggest Afro hairdo I had ever seen, sitting on an orange crate. He was peering at me over his wire-rimmed glasses as if he'd never seen a White man in the lobby of a Black radio station before. I nodded and said "Hello." That was his cue.

He slid the orange crate close to the sofa I was sitting on. He was so tall that even though he was sitting on an orange crate and the couch I was sitting on was much higher, he towered over me and had to bend down to talk to me.

"Are you Dr. King's lawyer?" he asked.

"No."

"His manager?"

"No, I'm just a volunteer for civil rights people, and I was asked to drive Dr. King to the studio this evening.

"That's all you do?"

"No, I have a job," I said, "I'm the merchandising and advertising manager for Sears, Roebuck and Company." That piqued his interest.

"Really? You're an advertising manager for Sears?" I nodded. He smiled.

"Listen, I've got to broadcast the midnight news, but I'll be right out. Do you want to go have a drink?"

"Sure," I responded.

After he finished the news, he drove his car. I followed him in mine to a restaurant/bar on the South Side called Flukies, which served a nice middle-class crowd.

"My name is Don Cornelius," he said, "I do the midnight news for WVON."

"So I gathered." I said, "I'm George O'Hare."

We ordered drinks. Don wanted to know how I met Dr. King and how I got involved in the Civil Rights Movement. After we had covered every aspect of the Movement, we moved on to other topics.

"I used to be a cop," he told me. That was hard for me to believe.

"I would've pegged you for a radio announcer," I said. He had a deep, baritone voice.

"Yeah, some of my friends told me I had a face for radio," he joked.

Don Cornelius was really a very handsome young man with a great personality. "You ever hear of Bill "Doc" Lee?" he asked. I told him I didn't know Bill "Doc" Lee personally, but I. like everyone else had heard of him. He was the religious and gospel radio personality for WVON. His voice was heard everyday introducing the records as they were played. He also conducted interviews and was the announcer for live commercials. But the story that everyone associated with his name was about how people with ailments would call "Doc" during his broadcast and he would pray their troubles away. Callers would phone the station later and report how "Doc" helped them get well.

Don told me that when he was a cop, he stopped "Doc" Lee once for speeding. "As I was giving him a warning, he interrupted me and said, 'Young man, you've got a great voice. You should be on the radio.' Then he gave me his card and told me to come to WVON for an audition. I auditioned, and they put me on a five-minute midnight news show."

"So do you have any thoughts of becoming a radio Deejay like Daddy-O Daylie or Herb Kent?" I asked him.

"Not at all," he said.

Then he pulled his bar stool closer as if he was getting ready to tell me some mind-blowing secret. "I have this idea," he whispered, "I want to have a TV show, you know, a Negro version of Dick Clark's American Bandstand."

I just shook my head sadly and said, "It'll never happen,"

"Why not?"

"Because you're Black. Look at what happened to Nat King Cole. Everybody loved listening to his music when they didn't know he was Black. But when he got that TV show, and White people saw he was Black, they canceled the show as soon as the contract was up."

"But at least they gave him a show," Don said. "That's all I need is a chance. Mine would be different. It would be great!"

I didn't want my new friend wasting his thoughts on a hopeless dream. "It will never happen," I repeated.

Flukie's Bar and Restaurant closed at two o'clock in the morning, so we left there, and I followed Don to the Tiger Lounge, another elite Chicago South Side Bar on Seventy-Ninth and Cottage Grove. The Tiger Lounge stayed open until four o'clock in the morning, and we stayed there until they closed. We exchanged numbers when we left the Tiger Lounge and promised to remain in touch with each other.

I enjoyed Don Cornelius' friendship immensely. I called him my drinking buddy; we both liked bars, and we both enjoyed talking. Don also had a great sense of humor.

I'll never forget the time I had dinner at Don's house. After I was seated at the dinner table, Don said, "My wife, Dolores, and I have a great treat for you, George." I wondered what it could be…a steak dinner? Maybe lobster. It wasn't either. Don's wife, Dolores, came into the dining room with a big plate of little white "rubbery looking things" which I later found out were chitterlings. As I sat there looking at them and wondering if they tasted as bad as they looked and smelled, Dolores said, "Would you like some chitterlings?" "Oh, I never had any, but I'd love to try them," I said. I had heard Negroes talk about chitterlings, pronounced "chitlins," and once again my crazy curiosity had gotten the best of me. Plus, I didn't think it would be polite to turn down a meal offered when you're a guest in someone's home. I picked one up with my fork and gingerly placed it in my mouth. I decided that it must be an acquired taste and I doubted seriously whether I would ever acquire it. I thought if I chewed it quickly and swallowed it whole, holding my breath in the process, maybe I could eat fast and finish before my taste buds were too severely assaulted. However, there was no hurrying when it came to chewing these little rubbery pieces of pig's intestines. After what felt like a lifetime, I managed to get them all down. I was hoping the tears I felt in my eyes weren't visible, when Don's wife said, "How'd you like them, George?" "Oh, delicious," I lied as I reached for a beer to wash out the taste. "Good, have some more," she said as she plopped another plateful of chitterlings in front of me. I sat there in stunned silence for a minute, and then reluctantly reached for my fork steeling myself for a second tortuous ordeal, at which point Don couldn't hold back the laughter any longer. He was laughing so hard he was almost in tears as he took the plate away from me.

*My Uncle Lou O'Hare. The most racist man I knew
and he taught me to be a racist.*

My Uncle Anderson "Husk" O'Hare,
the "Genial Gentleman of the Air."

My demonstrations of Sears' appliances were always entertaining.

Meeting the Reverend Dr. Martin Luther King, Jr.,
who became a good friend, was a turning point in my life.

My mentor, friend, soul mate, advisor, Dick Gregory.
Here we are with Martin Luther King III.

As advertising manager at Sears I met a lot of celebrities such as the
great musician, Ramsey Lewis, pictured here with Dick Gregory and me.

*My friend, the great singer, Tony Bennett, at a club with
my beautiful wife, Jean and me.*

*Father George Clements was the first Black Catholic Priest I ever met.
Here we are with his mentee and protégé, Father Michael Pfleger and others.*

Lou Gossett portrayed Father Clements in The Father Clements Story.
Father Clements also brought his sister on the set.

Actor, Ron McClarty played me in The Father Clements Story.

*Malcolm Jamal Warner portrayed Joey, Father Clements' first adopted son
in The Father Clements Story.*

*Sun-Times Columnist Irv Kupcinet of "Kup's Column" became a dear friend.
His column brought local and national attention to Dr. King and
the Civil Rights Movement.*

I helped "Kup" promote his annual Purple Hearts Cruise as a tribute to veterans.

After meeting the Honorable Minister Louis Farrakhan,
I became a frequent attendee at his meetings.

Alderman Eugene Sawyer, who became Mayor Eugene Sawyer after Harold's death, became a good friend.

After retiring from Sears, I became a motivational speaker and frequently spoke at Wright Junior College.

As a motivational speaker, my favorite audiences
were the elementary school children.

Dick Gregory once told me to "Fake it 'til you make it" I liked that slogan so much I
even had "Fake it 'til you make it" t-shirts made.

Father Clements and I are still best friends to this day.
Renault Robinson (pictured on my right) is one of the founders of
the African American Police League.

Here I am with my wonderful family, my three sons, George III,
Bob and Mike and their wives and my beloved wife, Jean.

*My sons, George III and Michael, and I attended Father Clements
60-years as a priest celebration.*

*Dick Gregory performed in Chicago three months before his death. I didn't know
that would be our last photograph together. May this wonderful soul Rest in Peace.*

CHAPTER 12

No More X's

"The time is always right to do what is right."
–Rev. Dr. Martin Luther King, Jr.

I told Dick Gregory about my dinner at Don's and through laughter he said, "Well George, you've been initiated. You're one of us now." To Gregory, that was a joke; but to my White neighbors, friends, and coworkers, it was a reality. They felt like I was hanging out with "those people" to the point that I was in danger of becoming like them, whatever in their minds "becoming like them," consisted of. The constant criticism became a part of my daily existence, especially from the other Sears, Roebuck managers, who couldn't understand why I was always hanging out with "those people."

To tell the truth, as much as I enjoyed my new friends and being a part of the Civil Rights Movement, I also felt uncomfortable. The thought of just getting out of the Civil Rights Movement occurred to me more than once. *Was it worth it? Would it be better if I just stayed away from the Black community and began to act like an average middle-class Irish Catholic White guy was supposed to act? Maybe instead of going to the Black community when I got off work, I should go to my middle-class suburban home and my White wife and kids; maybe then I wouldn't be in constant danger of losing my job or losing my friends.*

I sat in my office in deep thought, on the verge of giving in to the desires of my fellow managers, when the ringing of the phone brought me back to reality. The intercom buzzed. "It's Mr. Metcalf," my secretary reported. *Too late,* I thought. *He's going to fire me.* I picked up the phone. "George, meet me on the third floor in the lobby underneath the stairwell by the cashier's department." *Fine. At least he wants to fire me in private.*

I went to the third floor in the lobby ready to tell Mr. Metcalf that I was willing to stay out of the Black community if only he would allow me to keep my job.

"How're you doing?"

"Fine, Mr. Metcalf." *Just a little nervous about the possibility of losing my job at Sears that I love so much.*

"Having any trouble at the store?"

"What kind of trouble, Sir?"

"You know, are any of your fellow Sears's employees and managers riding you about associating with those Negroes?

"Well, yes sir, I get it every day. They tell me 'don't go around those Negroes.' They call me nigger-lover."

"Well George, don't mind them. I approve of what you're doing, so you just keep it up. If anybody gives you a hard time, let me know."

Shocked! Surprised! Overwhelmed! Relieved! All of those words and then some couldn't come close to describe the way I was feeling. It was as if a ten-ton weight had been lifted from my shoulders. After that, I had no more thoughts about leaving the Movement. If the Chairman of the Board of Sears gave his blessings, then there was nothing anyone else could say. I was free to love any Black person in the world that I wanted to love! Thank You, Jesus!

Not long after that, the managers stopped complaining about me hanging around "those people" and began asking if I knew of any Black people they could hire. All of the protests, marches, and boycotts were starting to make a difference. Dr. King, as well as Malcolm X, Jesse Jackson and other Black leaders did a great job of putting old Jim Crow on his deathbed. Now, I'm not saying racism no longer existed. There were still a lot of ignorant people who didn't like anyone unless they happened to have a skin color the same as or similar to theirs. However, there were companies like Sears that realized they could no longer uphold the racist tradition of hiring only White people. They had to join the many others who began labeling themselves as "equal employment opportunity companies."

"George, do you think you can hire a Negro secretary?" Mr. Metcalf asked me one day. "Sure," I said. I hung up the phone and called Dick Gregory.

"Mr. Metcalf wants me to hire a Negro secretary."

"That's great!"

I responded, "But what if she can't spell or take dictation? How am I going to get my letters typed?" For all the time I had spent in the Black community, I was still hanging on to some of the racist stereotypes I learned as a kid.

"Where'd you get that racist idea?" Gregory laughed, "Listen, you go and look through applications of individuals who were turned down for jobs at Sears, and I'll bet you'll find a Black secretary with skills and brains. Don't be surprised if she has three or four degrees and is much smarter than you."

"But if they're that smart and have all those degrees, why would they apply to be a secretary at Sears?" I asked.

"Because you racist White people won't hire them in the positions they're qualified for," said Gregory.

I thought about the big "X"s I had been taught to put in the upper left-hand corner of applications to let the personnel department know the applicant was Black. There was probably a lot of great talent relegated to those "circular" files aka wastebaskets. Fortunately, they all didn't wind up in the wastebaskets ; there were some applications with x's in the corner still in the files. Race was still allowed as a question on employment applications and most of the applicants that checked "Negro" were either very qualified or over qualified for the positions for which they were applying. After admitting to myself that Dick Gregory was right again, I began pouring through the applications. One in particular caught my eye. The applicant, Betty Powe, had a college degree and spoke three languages fluently. I immediately called her in for an interview. As impressive as she was on paper, she was even more captivating in person. At that point, I stopped thinking that every intelligent Black person I met had to be an exception to the race. In fact, I was beginning to question all of the things Uncle Lou had fed into my little racist mind.

I wasn't the only one. A lot of White people stopped being so overtly racist because of Dr. King and the movement. Nevertheless, we knew in too many cases some racist views were so deeply embedded in people's minds, that they could only think of Black people as inferior.

Besides race discrimination, there was also a problem with gender disparities. There's a song by James Brown entitled, "It's a Man's World." I was guilty of singing that song myself. Back then our society could be defined as a man's world, and Sears was one of the biggest culprits. The salespeople making big money at Sears were always men, never women. They used to call it the "good ole' boy's network." The only women who worked for Sears were the secretaries.

All that changed when a woman did the unheard of; she applied for a sales job at Sears. The Sears all-male upper management was baffled. "What are we going to do with a woman?" Mr. Metcalfe asked. They couldn't turn her away since Sears was now an "equal employment opportunity company." "Put her in stoves," I suggested, "All women cook." Well, she did such a great job selling Sears Kenmore stoves; they placed her in the Kenmore automatic washing machines and sewing machines department. She excelled in those departments, too. Eventually, women became some of Sears' top and greatest salespersons.

In 1965 the Government's Equal Employment Opportunity Commission (EEOC) was created as a significant part of the Civil Rights Bill. It required American businesses to stop discriminating against anyone because of their race, age, or gender.

"Hey, George O'Hare!"

I turned to see who was calling me. Speaking of racists, the Sears manager who was running toward me was one of the most racist people I had ever met. He had also been one of my most vocal critics, always telling me about the price I would have to pay for hanging around "those people."

"Say, George, I need to hire about ten of 'those people," he said.

Sadly, he was so racist he couldn't bring himself to simply say "those Black people," not that the N-word didn't quickly roll off his tongue, but most of my coworkers knew better than to use that word in my presence.

"What people?" I asked as if I didn't know.

"You know," he said.

"You want to hire a Black person?' I said. He couldn't say the word, and I wasn't going to force the issue. Let him be racist. At least he was giving Black individuals badly needed jobs.

"I need about ten of them," he said.

I said, "Sure," and immediately called Dick Gregory.

"You need some young, smart, up and coming Negroes," Gregory said, "And I'm going to introduce you to someone who can help you out."

So, Gregory took me around to meet a smart, up and coming young man named Fred Hampton.

Fred was the head of the Chicago Area Chapter of the Black Panther Party. Now a lot of people—Black and White—might say, "Oh, those Black Panthers were a group of hoodlums who wanted to kill White people, especially the White police." Nothing could be further from the truth. The Black Panther Party did a lot of good in the community, such as orchestrating a truce between the gangs so they would stop killing each other. (Wouldn't that be a beautiful thing today?) One of the Panther Party's main missions was to go to the Chicago Public Schools and serve hot breakfasts to the children because too many Black children did not get a good, warm breakfast at home. That certainly doesn't seem like a criminal action to me. But when Black people organized, no matter how much good they were doing, they were always called "radicals" and "militants" and were viewed as "threats."

Fred knew plenty of young college graduates who were unemployed because they were Black. He said, "George, I'll get you some people, but don't tell your bosses at Sears Roebuck, who you got them from, because if they learn its Fred Hampton, the Black Panther, they won't hire them."

Who would have thought I'd be discovering all of the things that I had in common with a Black man, but as Fred and I developed a friendship, I found I had a lot more in common with him than I did with many of my White friends.

We would visit each other's homes frequently since his home in Maywood was just a few minutes away from Bellwood. Fred and I could talk for hours, solving the world's problems. He wanted to help save Black people, especially the children and he was always coming up with a new idea for a program.

True to his word, Fred introduced me to ten young Black people and Sears hired every one of them. They did a super great job, and pretty soon the Sears' store managers were bombarding me with requests. "George, we need about ten more of them." "Ten more of what?" I asked. "Ten more Negroes; the one's you got us are great."

Thank God for the Civil Rights Movement and for that Movement to cause us, White people, to change our attitudes and begin to respect all, I repeat, ALL people—White, Black, Brown, Yellow, and Red—to help our great country be the land of equal opportunity.

One would have thought, with all of the changes that were coming about thanks to the Civil Rights Movement, that Jim Crow was dead. White corporations could no longer refuse to hire Black people just because of their gender or the color of their skin. In the South, it was no longer legal to lynch Black people. In spite of all these positive developments, racism still existed, especially in our nation's police departments. Too many Black people were still dying at the hands of White police officers.

You read about the acts of brutality practiced by white law enforcement against Black individuals, but it really hits home when it happens to someone you know and love. One cold December night in Chicago, States Attorney Edward Hanrahan ordered a group of policemen to raid the apartment shared by Fred Hampton and Mark Clark. The raid occurred in the early morning hours when Mark and Fred were sleeping. Fred and Mark were assassinated, murdered in cold blood while they slept. At first, Hanrahan and top police officials claimed that it was a shootout. But that turned out to be a lie when it was discovered that all of the bullet holes were going into the apartment, none were coming out. They couldn't have been firing at the police because they were sleeping.

The death of Fred Hampton and Mark Clark was a great loss for the Black community. Fred was a very conscientious person who wanted to make things better. My grandmother often talked about mortal and venial sins, but for such an incredibly smart and promising young man to be taken from this world just because he was trying to help his people; now that's a real mortal sin.

Even before this senseless murder occurred, a group of Black police officers, led by Renault Robinson, who we called "Reggie," and Edward Palmer, whose nickname was "Buzz," formed an organization called the African American Patrolman's League. After women joined the group, the organization became the African American Police League.

These young male and female police officers were concerned about police brutality. They weren't alone in their concerns. Father George Clements was very outspoken about his opposition to the tactics used by Chicago Police and he spoke forcefully against their treatment of Black citizens during an interview on Wesley South's "Hotline." Renault Robinson and Buzz Palmer heard that show and Renault immediately called Father Clements and asked if he would meet with their group. Father Clements agreed to the meeting. If Renault and Buzz had been impressed with what Father Clements said on the radio, they were ten times more impressed after meeting with him in person.

By the close of the meeting, Renault and Buzz had asked Father Clements to be their spiritual advisor and Father Clements had accepted. Renault was also a devout Catholic and he and his wife, Annette, were members of Father Clements's congregation at Holy Angels Catholic Church. Their children went to Holy Angels School.

I soon began volunteering to do public relations work for the Afro-American Police League, and after awhile police brutality was no longer a secret. The entire city became aware of the horrible reality of what was going on between the Chicago Police and the Black community. Unfortunately many Whites didn't care. They still saw every White policeman as the personification of "Officer Friendly" and every Black victim as a thug who deserved to be assaulted or killed at the hands of these "fine officers."

Renault Robinson's Police Department superiors didn't know what to do with him. They felt he was rebellious, which he was, but only for a worthy cause and in a positive way. When they began mandating the equipping of all police cars in the Black communities with very visible combat rifles on the dashboards inside their vehicles, Renault balked. He refused to allow them to put an assault rifle in his car. The commander demanded Renault comply with his order to place the combat rifle in the automobile where it was visible for all to see. So, Renault, knowing he had no choice, went to the loading dock where the rifles were held. Suddenly there was a loud boom. Everyone came out to see what had happened. Renault had shot one of the rifles into the ground. He got his point across and also got reprimanded in a very novel way.

In retaliation for what Renault's superiors thought was an act of insubordination, the Commander assigned Renault to foot patrol in the alley behind police headquarters. Although I joked about Renault patrolling the building that housed the most corrupt people in Chicago, the Chicago Police, I promptly told my friend Irv Kupcinet about Renault's assignment to "alley duty." The next day a picture of Renault Robinson patrolling the alleyway appeared in the *Chicago Sun-Times*. One of the many people who saw the article and was appalled by it was an excellent attorney by the name of Robert "Bob" Howard. Bob joined Renault Robinson and Howard Saffold, another Black police officer and one of the founding members of the African American Police League, in developing a citywide coalition and organizing a class action lawsuit on behalf of victims of police brutality. That resulted in the formation of the Chicago Police Department's Office of Professional Standards.

Afterward, we thought things would change, but unfortunately, that did not happen. Today there is just as much, if not more, police brutality—especially against our Black and brown citizens.

Father Clements's connection with the Afro-American Police League proved helpful in more ways than one. On one occasion, Renault learned that the Chicago Police were planning to set up Dick Gregory with drugs. The limo driver hired to take Gregory to Chicago's O'Hare Airport had the drugs. If everything had gone as planned, Dick Gregory's career and reputation would have been destroyed. It was fortunate that Renault, as a member of the Police Force, heard of the plan and was able to get word to Father Clements. Father Clements immediately alerted Gregory, who changed his plans and stayed at the hotel instead of taking the limo to the airport.

CHAPTER 13

Racism Kills

"Assassination is the extreme form of censorship"
—GEORGE BERNARD SHAW

In those days, there were plenty of White folks who, like my Uncle Lou, abhorred the idea of integration or equality, and they certainly didn't want the masses exposed to the truth of what was happening in our nation. They targeted people like Dick Gregory and Dr. Martin Luther King and other Civil Rights Leaders. They would rather take a life than live in harmony with people of another color.

Dr. King knew that what he was doing was extremely dangerous. But he also knew that he was doing what had to be done. Riding home some nights from a local civil rights meeting or rally, Dr. King would sometimes talk about the Movement, and about the deep-seated racism that existed throughout the country.

"The irony is that there are very powerful people with a lot of money who don't care what color your skin is," Dr. King said one night as we sat in the car. I thought they would be the most racist ones, but Dr. King explained they only used racism as a tool to keep the races divided. "Only one percent of the entire population of the United States controls all the power and all the wealth," he said. "As long as the poor and lower middle-class Whites hate Negroes, and as long as Negroes resent racist Whites, the ninety-nine percent will never come together to challenge the power of the one percent, and that's what they're banking on." Then he told me something very profound. "That's why they don't attack Negroes for talking about Negro issues, but let one of us start talking about poor and powerless Whites joining the impoverished and powerless Negroes, and they would try to shut us down and shut us out very quickly." "Imagine." He said, "If instead of fighting each other, poor White people and poor Black people could come together and demand their fair share of wealth and power. Just imagine if all the poor and other disenfranchised people, Black and White, joined forces to fight this small percentage of individuals who are controlling their lives. What would happen if White people stopped hating Black people but instead, joined with them in boycotting and protesting the greedy and powerful one percent?"

I thought about that. "It would be great, but I guess it'll never happen," I said.

"Never say never, George," Dr. King said to me,

I thought about that conversation a few weeks later when Dr. King started making plans to go to Memphis, Tennessee, to join a group of Black garbage workers. They asked Dr. King to come to Memphis and help them fight for equal wages for their work. Dr. King took this as an opportunity to organize, not a Black People's March, but a "Poor People's March." The purpose of the march was to bring the Black sanitation workers and the White sanitation workers together and help them understand, as long as they continued to fight each other, they would remain poor and the powerless.

We spoke briefly before he left for Memphis. I told him to have a safe trip and to be careful.Although I always encouraged him to have a safe trip and come back safely; that was the first time I said, "Be careful." The night before he left, he gave a very moving speech. He was getting threats about coming to Memphis, and I could tell by his words that those threats were on his mind. His words were hauntingly prophetic:

"Well, I don't know what will happen now. We've got some difficult days ahead. But it really doesn't matter with me now, because I've been to the mountaintop. And I don't mind. Like anybody, I would like to live a long life; longevity has its place. But I'm not concerned about that now. I just want to do God's will. And He's allowed me to go up to the mountain. And I've looked over. And I've seen the Promised Land. I may not get there with you. But I want you to know tonight, that we, as a people, will get to the Promised Land. So I'm happy, tonight. I'm not worried about anything. I'm not fearing any man. Mine eyes have seen the glory of the coming of the Lord!"

That was the last time I saw my friend and mentor, the Reverend Dr. Martin Luther King, Jr. On April 4, 1968, Dr. King's vision of bringing poor Whites and poor Blacks together was shattered by a bullet fired by a man named James Earl Ray, as Dr. King stood on the balcony of the Lorraine Hotel in Memphis, Tennessee. When I heard the news of his assassination; I was devastated. The sorrow and emptiness I felt was indescribable. What was more overwhelming was the terrible anger I felt.

Here I was, a 41-year-old White, Irish Catholic crying over the death of a Black Baptist preacher and angry at the racism that caused his death. I was struck with the realization that as a White man born and raised in the midst of the Jim Crow era, those same racist beliefs that caused a White supremacist to shoot and kill this man had been instilled in my own mind from my early childhood.

Life is not all happiness and joy. When a great person dies too soon, that brings on an inexplicable kind of sadness. When President Kennedy was assassinated, I mourned along with the rest of the world. When they assassinated Malcolm X, I was saddened, not only because of his death but because of the waste of so much brilliance. But neither Kennedy's death nor Malcolm X's can compare with the great loss I felt when Dr. King was killed in Memphis.

Here was a man I knew personally; a man who had made a great many positive changes for the good of this world in his short lifetime. We had, spent time together as I drove him from place to place, talking about everything. Dr.

King was well aware of the dangers associated with Civil Rights in this racist world, and he was keenly aware of the risk he was taking by introducing the concept of poor Whites and poor Blacks coming together in unity. At one time in a Chicago protest march, he was hit with a brick. He had been stabbed on a bus, and targeted, along with his family, and a bomb had been thrown into his home. The speech he made the night before his assassination seemed to eerily predict his death.

I can honestly say I loved Dr. King, not just because of what he did for me, but what he did for the world. I am so grateful for the wonderful memories of talking to King on the rides to his house or a radio interview, acting as his volunteer public relations person, marching with him, and going to hear his brilliant speeches. It thrilled me when I would take my son George with me to hear Dr. King, Dr. King would come down off the podium and grab my son's hand and bring him to the front to sit next to him.

I witnessed what being a part of the Movement and being close to Dr. King did for my very dear friend, Dick Gregory. When Gregory became part of Dr. King's nonviolent movement, he was in it 100 percent. I watched him evolve—physically and mentally. He stopped eating meat because he wanted nothing to do with anything that had been violently killed or had caused the death of another one of God's creatures. I watched him fast from food and water for days, weeks, and months at a time. Once I thought he was going to die because he had lost such a huge amount of weight by fasting for weeks.

Father Clements and I comforted each other and shared our feelings about Dr. King's tragic death. Father Clements told me how Dr. King's death changed his life forever.

"George," he said, "I was no longer a Black man striving to be a good White Priest, but at that time I looked in the mirror and saw a Black man, so I became a Black man striving to be a good Black priest."

Father Clements had already become embroiled in the civil rights movement because of his good friend, Dr. King. He marched with Dr. King in Selma, Alabama, and he was with Dr. King in Washington when he gave the "I have a Dream" Speech. But Father Clements said, "Something happened the day Dr. King died, and I knew I would never be the same again."

He told me that he was at St. Dorothy's Catholic Church when upon hearing of Dr. King's assassination he ran into the Church to pray.

"George," he said, "As I looked at the statues of the saints, something hit me, and I realized Dr. King is the same as all these other saints."

He told me that thought stayed with him, and later, when he became Pastor of Chicago's Holy Angels Church, he moved one of the statutes on the altar to another location and replaced it with a statue of Dr. Martin Luther King. Cardinal Cody was furious when he heard about it.

"You can't put a Baptist Preacher there," Cody exclaimed, "The only statues in the church are those of saints."

Father Clements explained to Cardinal Cody that during the Middle Ages; saints became saints by the acclamation of the people. "All the people have acclaimed that Rev. Dr. Martin Luther King, Jr. is a saint," he said.

Of course, that explanation didn't help matters. To say the Cardinal was enraged would be putting it mildly. He questioned whether Father Clements had lost his mind by calling a Protestant minister a saint. He didn't just ask, he demanded that Father Clements take down the Dr. King statue immediately. However, Father Clements stood his ground. Father Clements not only refused to take it down, he told Cardinal Cody if he wanted it down; then he would have to take it down himself.

"You can send someone down here to do it," Father Clements said, "But I'm not responsible for their safety here in the 'hood." Cardinal Cody was smart enough to know that if the news got out that he made a Black priest take down a statue of the Reverend Dr. Martin Luther King Jr., the recently assassinated martyr and hero of the Black community; it would make him look terrible. So, the statue remained.

CHAPTER 14

Soul Train

"Help others to achieve their dreams and you will achieve yours."
–LES BROWN

Don Cornelius became my friend because I took Dr. King to the Wesley South show and Don was there, waiting to do the midnight news. We remained good friends. As pessimistic as I was then about Don's dream of having his African American version of American Bandstand on TV, Don continued to believe that someday, somehow, some way it would happen. No matter what we did or what we talked about, the conversation would always come around to his dream of a Negro American Bandstand. Dick Clark's American Bandstand only played White Rock and Roll music. Don's version would play Rhythm and Blues and Soul music. He visualized his TV show as being a place where Black artists and Black teenage dancers could appear and be seen and heard by TV audiences nationwide.

Once or twice Don had stopped by my office at Sears near closing time to see if I wanted to go for a drink, which I usually did. He seldom showed up earlier in the day, except on one occasion. I happened to be on the phone talking to Mr. Metcalf when Don came into my office. With Don was Wesley South, the host of the popular WVON Radio Talk Show entitled "Hotline," and also WVON's Executive Vice President. Before I finished my conversation with Mr. Metcalf, Don whispered in my ear the name of the show would be called "Soul Train." I hurried up and finished the call and told my secretary to hold my calls. I sensed this was something crucial.

"We just signed a contract with WCIU, the local station," Don said, "They are going to air my show!" Don was so excited I expected to see him jump up and down any minute. I was excited for him, but I still couldn't resist the temptation to rib him a little bit.

"What show?"

"*Soul Train*!" Don said, repeating the name he had whispered into my ear. I had no idea what "Soul Train" meant, but it was indeed a catchy show title.

Wesley South piped in, "Now all we need is a sponsor to pay for the airtime," I knew the next question before he even asked. "Do you think Sears would sponsor it? It's only a hundred dollars a week for thirteen weeks."

Fate is a funny thing. When Don and Wesley South came to my office, I was just finishing a phone call with Mr. Metcalfe in which he expressed his concern about the slow movement of the 45-RPMs and the albums in our Phonograph record inventory. Before I hung up, Mr. Metcalf had asked me to think of some promotion or program that would bring people into Sears to buy our records. I told my secretary to get Mr. Metcalf back on the phone. "Mr. Metcalf," I said, "a friend of mine has an idea for a televised music and dance show, and if Sears would sponsor it, I'm sure people would come to the stores to buy our records."

Timing is everything. If I had brought the idea to Mr. Metcalfe any other time, chances are he would have rejected it. But on that day and at that time he had a specific problem and Don Cornelius and Wesley South showed up with a solution.

"What would you call the show?" Mr. Metcalfe asked. "*Soul Train,*" I said. After a pause, Mr. Metcalfe asked, "What does *Soul Train* mean?"

I had to admit that I had no idea what it meant, but Mr. Metcalfe agreed that it was a catchy title. "Maybe we can try it out for a thirteen-week contract," he said.

Don was beside himself. His dream was coming true.

Don called on his old friend, Clinton Ghent, to help put a mock show together. In the early 60's Don and Clinton were "regulars" at Budland, a nightclub on 63rd and Cottage Grove, downstairs in the Pershing Hotel. Back then Black young adults and older Black teens who loved to dance frequented Budland. "Clint and I were there every Tuesday night, right up on the dance floor," said Don, "And nobody could dance like Clinton with his short body and long legs."

"You probably don't know anything about 63rd and Cottage Grove," Don said.

What did he say that for? I told Don about my father's restaurant and bar; the Tivoli Tap Room, located right across the street from Budland. "Can you believe 63rd and Cottage Grove was all-White back then?" I said. Don could and did believe.

Don asked Clinton if he could round up some dancers to help the potential sponsors envision the show. Although the dancers in the video were older than the ones Don said would be in the show, it gave us a good idea of how the show would look. My bosses liked it, and so, *Soul Train* aired live on the local Chicago TV station, WCIU, with Don Cornelius hosting it.

Soul Train was an immediate success. It even beat the ratings of the number one White music show which had been the most popular show in that time slot. The advertising worked. People were lined up at Sears buying the records they heard on *Soul Train*.

Viewers watched the Sears-sponsored *Soul Train* show on TV and listened to the Negro Deejays on radio. The top three were, Daddy O'Daylie, Herb Kent "the Kool Gent," and Sid McCoy. Sid McCoy would start his broadcast with, "Hey, hey Old Bean and you, too Baby, this is Sid McCoy, the Real McCoy."

In between playing the hits, Herb Kent would entertain his listening audience with characters he made up, like "the Wahoo Man," purple-hat-wearing-Rudolph, or a hilarious character he called "Barbeque Bobby." At the end of each of his shows, he'd always play a beautiful gospel song called *Open Our Eyes*.

It became known throughout Sears that any product one of the Deejays promoted would become an instant best seller.

One of the store managers was having trouble selling washing machines, so Mr. Metcalf told him to start advertising on *Soul Train* and other Black radio stations. The store manager placed advertising with WVON. Herb Kent did a great job of promoting Sears' washing machines. He told his listeners,

"If you want something cleaned, just go to Sears and get a Kenmore Washing Machine. It's perfect for cleaning everything! The other day I cleaned a batch of Chitlins"

Customers began coming into the store looking for the "Chitlin Cleaner" they had heard advertised on Herb Kent's show.

Soul Train was off the charts. Some Hollywood producers saw the show and liked it and asked Don to bring it to Hollywood. Clinton Ghents became the host of our local Chicago show for a short time until he joined Don to do the national show in California. I tried to get my bosses to agree to sponsor the national show, but they declined. I think they missed a super great opportunity. A local Black-owned hair care company, Johnson Products, sponsored *Soul Train* which, along with Johnson's Hair Care products, gained national recognition.

In a way, Dr. King was responsible for Don Cornelius' dream becoming a reality. If I hadn't taken Dr. King to the radio station and met Don Cornelius, he never would have shared his vision, and I would never have been able to get Sears' National Advertising Department to sponsor it.

CHAPTER 15

Stepin Fetchit

"When people rely on surface appearances and false racial stereotypes rather than in-depth knowledge of others at the level of the heart, mind and spirit, their ability to assess and understand people accurately is compromised."
–JAMES A. FORBES

When my father, George O'Hare, Sr., named his black Great Dane watchdog "Stepin Fetchit," he unwittingly and unknowingly made a racist statement that had a significant impact on my young mind. If Stepin Fetchit represented all Black people—then can you blame a White person for thinking Black people are good for nothing and shiftless?

Months after Rev. Dr. Martin Luther King's assassination, CBS produced a documentary called, *Of Black America*. Bill Cosby narrated the portion of the documentary which was about how Hollywood had portrayed Blacks, especially men. That segment was called, *Black History: Lost, Stolen or Strayed* and one of the most scathing critiques in it was Cosby's very brutal evaluation of Stepin Fetchit's performances. In introducing those performances, Cosby said: "The tradition of the lazy, stupid, crap-shooting, chicken-stealing Negro was popularized by an actor by the name of Lincoln Monroe Andrew Perry , known in movies as Stepin Fetchit. This "cat" made $2 million in five years in the middle 1930's and everybody who saw the movies laughed at Stepin Fetchit. Too bad he was as good at it as he was."

Bill Cosby narrated some short clips from "Stepin Fetchit's" movies, noting, "He played in films with other actors who were as all-American as Mom's Raspberry Jelly. If they accepted the stereotype, how bad could it be?"

If that wasn't disparaging enough, he also showed a clip of "Step" with Little Shirley Temple. "The cute little White girl was brave and fierce in the face of danger. The Big Black man was stupid and cowardly," Cosby said.

I hadn't seen a "Stepin Fetchit" movie since my childhood. I wondered how Stepin Fetchit must have felt about such a devastating review of his life's work. Months later, I found out.

Dick Gregory phoned me and said, "George, I need you to do me a favor." "Sure, Gregory," I said, "You name it." He told me he needed me to help his friend, Lincoln Perry, who was now living in Chicago. "He's the guy that played Stepin Fetchit in the movies," Gregory explained, "but now he's totally depressed. I would like you to work with him, publicize him, and talk to him. Do whatever you can do. Just make the dude happy!"

At that time, I wondered if the CBS Documentary and Cosby's merciless criticism of Step's performances had anything to do with Stepin Fetchit's depression. I learned that it had everything to do with it.

After seeing the documentary, Step's son, Donald, who was a Black nationalist, turned on Step. He couldn't deal with the thought of his father having created the stereotypes that made Black people look no good and lazy.

It appeared Step's son wasn't the only one who turned on him; the whole world seemed to have turned against him. People who used to be friends were shunning him. Associates were embarrassed by him. Even a lot of his former White friends were upset. They felt like he had pulled the wool over their eyes. You could count the few people on one hand who still had some respect for him.

Step had been scheduled to co-star in a sitcom with Flip Wilson, a new young comedian. After the fallout of the documentary, Wilson did the show on his own.

To make matters worse, Step's son Donald had gone off the deep end and drove up the Pennsylvania Turnpike shooting people. He injured fifteen people and killed three, including his wife. Then he fatally shot himself. I could imagine how devastated Step was. I was devastated just hearing about it.

I called Father Clements, and we went to see "Step" at Chicago's Mercy Hospital. After his release, we continued to visit him at the public housing complex in which he lived. (Today, that public housing complex has been named the Lincoln Perry Homes.) Step didn't have very much of anything in his little kitchenette apartment, just a sofa, a few chairs, and a black and white TV with a lousy, fuzzy picture screen. All the money he earned over his many years of enjoying Hollywood fame and fortune was gone. The only thing left was a big trunk with all kinds of memorabilia from years ago. He proudly showed those trinkets and posters from the past to anyone who visited him.

Step wanted the world to know he wasn't the kind of person Bill Cosby claimed he was. He would write things down on sheets of paper about how famous he used to be, along with the names of the movies he had starred in and the movie stars he knew. Then he would stand on the street corner, handing out copies to passers-by. He was obsessed.

Some of his so-called friends thought it would be in the best interest of "Step" to commit him to an "old folks" home. Step wanted no part of that, and I agreed that an icon who gave so much of himself to the world should not end his days in a nursing home.

Step had to go to court to fight for his freedom, and Father Clements and I went with him. He answered every one of the judge's questions in an intelligent and sane manner. It certainly wasn't a question of his sanity, maybe it was his age that prompted the judge to ask, "Does this man have a legal guardian?" I looked around the courtroom to see if anyone was going to step forward, then I felt Father Clements gently nudging me with his elbow and motioning for me to step up and claim this responsibility. To everyone's surprise, including mine, on that day I became the legal guardian of Lincoln Perry aka Stepin Fetchit.

Step never really got over what he felt CBS did to his image by airing the documentary. He filed a $3 million lawsuit against CBS, which excluded Bill Cosby as a co-defendant. Step did not blame Cosby, nor did he see the comedian as the source of the wrong. As far he was concerned, it was CBS, Twentieth Century-Fox, and the Xerox Corporation, that were responsible for distorting his image. "Cosby was just a soldier," he once said. "He was not the general." But he also said, "A few years ago, Cosby wouldn't have been able to be where he is—I was the one who made it possible for him."

The judge dismissed the lawsuit, saying Stepin Fetchit" was a public figure subject to have people talk about him. That documentary not only hurt his pride, but it also damaged his relationships—and his life.

Gregory had told me to do some public relations for "Step," which was right up my alley. I contacted some of my friends, and since I was doing the senior citizen circuit at the time, I encouraged Step to come and speak at clubs and homes for the elderly. "Get on the stage," I told him. "Tell your life story. Tell them who you are and what you've done." That's just what he did, and the audiences loved it. Step was beginning to feel good about himself again.

When it came to religion, Step was very devout and a much better Catholic than I had ever been. Although I thought the bible was beautiful, and the prayers were excellent, I couldn't see how it helped poor people. That's the one thing that bothered me about the Catholic Church, because Jesus did say, "Help the poor." The Catholic Church's apparent apathy toward the poor didn't interfere with Step's steadfast commitment to the faith. He took Holy Communion every single morning. In Catholicism, that was called being a "daily communicant."

Once when an illness brought him to the Charity Ward in Cook County Hospital, Father Clements and I went to visit him. As soon as we arrived, he asked me to find out what time they would begin serving Communion. I asked the nurse who explained that Cook County Hospital did not serve Holy Communion. Irate and upset, Step immediately phoned City Hall and asked to speak to Mayor Richard J. Daley. Not everyone could speak directly to the Mayor, but Step, being who he was, was instantly connected. "Did you know Cook County Hospital doesn't serve Communion?" he asked the Mayor, who was a Catholic also. Mayor Daley said he didn't know that, but from that day on,

Cook County Hospital served Holy Communion to any patient that requested it.

A couple of years later, "Step" had a bad stroke that caused him to fall and break his jaw and left him paralyzed on one side of his body. As soon as I heard about it, I rushed over to Michael Reese Hospital. When I entered his room, Step was having a conversation with a man who was standing by his bed. I felt like I was invading a private conversation, but I didn't want to just walk out either, so I stood and waited. Finally, the man said to Step, "I love you, and I'll see you tomorrow." As he walked out of the room, he beckoned for me to follow him. Once outside of the room, he said,

"That's an incredible man."

. "Yes, he is," I said, openly staring at this man. "Excuse me," I said, "But you look and talk just like John Wayne, the movie star."

"Yes, that's me," he admitted. He told me he was going to do everything he could to help "Step." "I owe everything I am to that man," he said.

Wayne explained that when he was on the University of Southern California's football team, the team was to appear in a scene in a movie called the *Salute,* which starred Stepin Fetchit. "I wanted to find a way to get close to the director," Wayne said. "So I got a job as a prop man in the movie and was assigned as "Step's" wardrobe man. When I told "Step" I wanted to be an actor, he introduced me to the director, John Ford, who promised to make me a star and he did. I owe it all to my friend, Lincoln Perry."

Michael Reese wasn't a charity hospital like Cook County Hospital. "Step" was still in the same boat—he had no money, and he had a big hospital bill. He also had a lot of friends who loved him. One was the dancer and singer, Ben Vereen. Vereen arranged a birthday salute for "Step" at the Arie Crown Theater.

Even though "Step" was in a wheelchair and couldn't move his arm, he was happier than I'd seen him in a long time. The event was great; celebrities and other friends of Step had packed the place, and all the performances were fantastic. Stevie Wonder had written a song especially for "Step." A singer by the name of Lovelace Watkins did a rendition of *Old Man River* that he dedicated to the man of the hour, Lincoln Monroe Andrew Perry, aka Stepin Fetchit.

Before Step passed away, he and I had become very good friends. I once shared with him a piece of my childhood. "My father had a big Great Dane dog," I told him, "and do you know what his name was?" "Step" admitted he had no idea, so I told him, "Stepin' Fetchit." He got a good laugh out of that.

CHAPTER 16

Black Man of the Month

"There would never be a civil rights movement ever if it hadn't been for the fact that we had many, many, many White people who stood up behind our Black people and our Latino people, and who fought for our rights, and don't you dare leave those White people out of this struggle."
–FATHER GEORGE CLEMENTS

ather Clements was usually available to accompany me whenever I was going to an event, or visiting "Stepin Fetchit," and I also made myself available whenever he wanted me for anything. All he had to do was call, which is exactly what he did one evening in April.

"George, I've got something to ask you."

"Go ahead, Father," I said. I knew whatever he asked me; my answer would be yes.

"No, no," he said, "I want to talk to you in person."

When I arrived at the Rectory, Father went right into his explanation;

"I try to find Black men in the Parish who help other Black people," he said, "and when I find that person, I give him the Black Man of the Month Award."

I nodded my head. "That's very commendable, Father," I said, wondering why he wanted to talk to me about this. *Maybe he wanted me to recommend someone worthy of that recognition.*

He continued, "I present the award during regular Church service, and the recipients bring their whole family to watch them receive it."

I nodded and smiled. It was certainly an excellent idea to give men credit for helping others, but I continued to wonder what that had to do with me. *Perhaps write a press release about it? Maybe he wanted Kup to do a column about his next Black Man of the Month Award.*

"Here's what I'd like to do," Father said, "I'd like to make you the Black Man of the Month." Well, I surely didn't see that coming.

"Oh, no, Father, I couldn't accept that," I said.

"Well, I'm not going to force it on you, George," he responded, "It's your choice, and if you don't want to accept it that's okay."

My ego rose up in me and caused me to shout, "I'll take it!"

I wondered how my wife, Jean, would react to my acceptance of the award. I didn't have to wonder long—she was thrilled. God blessed me with a loving wife who was always supportive of me; even though she didn't agree with a lot of things I did. But this time she was in total agreement with her White, Irish Catholic husband being the recipient of the Black Man of the Month Award and that was critical to me.

Father Clements presented the award to me during a regular church service. When I walked up to the pulpit to accept it, I looked out into the congregation and saw my wife and three sons, George, Robert and Michael, smiling broadly. I could see the pride in their eyes, especially my wife's, as Father Clements handed me a beautiful oak and metal plaque and spoke of all the reasons he felt I was deserving of the award. The media was there also. Irv Kupcinet wrote an article about my receiving the Black Man of the Month Award. *Time Magazine,* said:

"The award honors outstanding contributions to the race, and it is presented by Holy Angel's Parish in a Black area of Chicago's South Side. The current Black Man of the Month is George O'Hare, a Sears, Roebuck executive who was awarded the

plaque for his work with the late Martin Luther King Jr. in Chicago and his efforts to improve education and other conditions in the city's ghettos. The fact that O'Hare is White did not trouble the parish. Pastor George Clements said, "Blackness is a way of life and not merely a skin color."(Time Magazine, May 1, 1972)

Shortly after receiving the award, I received a call from Sister Claudette Muhammad, Chief of Protocol for the Honorable Minister Louis Farrakhan. She told me that Minister Farrakhan had read the article in *Time Magazine* about how I was honored as "Black man of the month," and he was inviting me to dinner at his mansion to talk about the award and find out what led Father Clements to give it to me, a White man. I had heard Minister Farrakhan speak, but I never met him.

As soon as I hung up the phone, I called Dick Gregory. "I've been invited to Minister Louis Farrakhan's for dinner, should I accept?" "Yes, definitely," he said."I'd like to go, also."

Minister Farrakhan lives in the mansion that once belonged to the Honorable Elijah Muhammad. Sister Claudette met me at the door. The large basket of socks at the entrance and the shoes neatly lined up around it served to let guests know to remove their shoes. We followed Sister Claudette to the dining room which was dominated by the longest table I had ever seen. As we enjoyed the delicious meal and listened to this man's conversation about world peace, ending poverty, politics and of course, Civil Rights, I thought *if anyone doubts the intelligence of African Americans, they need only listen to the conversation of the Honorable Minister Louis Farrakhan for five minutes.* He was amazingly brilliant! Minister Farrakhan and Dick Gregory hit it off right away, and both Greg and I developed a close and lasting friendship with Minister Farrakhan. Recently, Minister Farrakhan gave a very eloquent eulogy at the memorial service for my beloved friend, Dick Gregory.

Minister Farrakhan was nothing like the "Jew-hater" the media tried to make him out to be. "Love your neighbors" wasn't just a cliché for the Minister. It was the way he lived his life, with love for everyone. As I listened to him, I thought about my dear Jewish friend, Irv Kupcinet. How I wished Kup was there to hear what I was hearing.

The time went by too quickly as we spent more than five hours listening to this Muslim, who was a giant of a man. Although that was my first time at the Minister's home, it wasn't the last. I attended many more dinners at the Minister's mansion and grew to love and respect him more with each visit. Sometimes Father Clements would join me, other times Dick Gregory and I would go to the Minister's home, and many times the three of us went together .Minister Farrakhan and I became friends to the point that he gave me his personal phone number so that I did not have to go through Sister Claudette each time I called him.

One evening, after I had visited with Minister Farrakhan and as I was preparing to leave, I said, "Minister Farrakhan, is it okay if I bring a friend of mine with me the next time I come?"

"Of course," he said, and then asked, "Who is it?"

When I told him it was Irv Kupcinet, the Minister said, "Do you think he will come?"

"Of course he will," I assured him. But the Minister didn't think so, and it turned out he was right. When I said to Kup that I'd like him to come with me to dinner at Minister Farrakhan's home, he flatly refused, saying he had no interest in meeting Louis Farrakhan. I called the Minister. Before I could get the words out of my mouth, he said,

"Kup is not coming."

"Yes," I said. "He said no."

"I didn't think he would come," the Minister said, quietly.

A couple of weeks later, Kup surprised me again. We were having lunch, doing our middle-of-the-week catch up, when he said, "You know what, George I would like to meet Minister Farrakhan." Just like that. I don't know what changed his mind and I didn't ask because it really didn't matter.

The Minister warmly welcomed Kup to his home. We had a great conversation at the dinner table and afterward, Kup thanked me for inviting him and said anytime the Minister would have us back, he'd love to go.

The next day, Kup wrote in his column, "*I met a man that I had never met before. Although I had spoken of him, I really didn't know him. He is a wonderful man and the meeting was set up by my friend, George O'Hare.*"

One evening after spending five or six hours with the Minister, he walked me to the door as he always did and said as he usually did, "Thank you for coming."

"You should thank me," I said, "after this great sacrifice I made."

"What sacrifice?" Minister Farrakhan asked puzzled.

"Why I went nearly six hours without having a beer," I said. (Alcohol of any kind is forbidden in the Islam religion.)

The Minister and I both got a good laugh out of that remark.

Besides abstaining completely from any alcoholic beverage, members of the Nation of Islam don't smoke either. In fact, they lead very religious lives, and they are all very committed to the principles and traditions of Islam.

Muhammad Ali committed to the Nation and changed his name to Ali from Cassius Clay. When he was Cassius Clay, I hated him. *How could this Negro go around saying "I'm the greatest?"* I wondered. *Greater than what? Than White people? No way!* Negroes were supposed to be humble. They were expected to know their place, which was and would always be beneath White people. That was the previous way of talking and the old mindset of George O'Hare—before I became a recovering racist. By the time I met and became a friend of Muhammad Ali, those racist thoughts had long been driven from my mind.

The word had gotten out about how Dick Gregory was helping people with a supplement he created called the 4X Formula. Impressed by what he had heard, Ali came to Gregory and asked for his help. He wanted to get back in shape so that he could make a comeback for the third time and win back his title from Leon Spinks. At first, it looked a little hopeless because Ali had gained an awful lot of weight and he just didn't have the energy and spark he had as a younger championship boxer.

All that began to change when Gregory started helping him with his diet. Of course, Gregory, being a runner, suggested running as the daily exercise for Ali. Gregory and Ali would drive their Rolls Royce's to Chicago's Jackson Park and run around the park every day. One day Gregory told me to come and ride with him to meet Ali for their daily run. He gave me a chore to do. While Gregory and Ali jogged along the Jackson Park trails, I drove alongside them in one of their Rolls Royce's with the towels. Afterwards, I became a part of their daily run. One day I would drive Gregory's

Rolls Royce, the next day I would drive Ali's, slowly around the park, always ready with the towels and water to cool down either or both of them when they came to the car to wipe the sweat or take a sip of water. I also had a spray bottle of water which I would spritz them with.

Ali was a wonderful person. And even though he didn't hold the title at that time, he was and would always be the champ as far as I was concerned. I no longer resented him saying he was the greatest because he truly was awesome in my mind. By calling himself the greatest, I believe a lot of African Americans learned its okay to think highly of themselves; they didn't have to be humble and go around with their heads down saying, "yassuh boss." Ali not only said he was great, but he showed how great he was in and outside of the ring, fight after fight.

Ali's greatest enemy wasn't Leon Spinks or any of his opponents in the ring—it was his love of junk food. Dick Gregory told him he would never get in shape if he didn't change his terrible eating habits and when his manager started booking fights for him again, he knew he couldn't trust himself to leave the junk food alone.

"Come on and go with me, Man," he said to Gregory, "Everything will be on me, and you'll get to see the world."

Gregory had pretty much seen the world, and he knew his schedule wouldn't allow him to travel with the Champ to keep him from eating himself out of shape again. "Listen," he said to Ali, "I'm going to send my White, Irish Catholic, racist friend, George O'Hare with you to make sure you don't eat any junk food." Wow! I was thrilled.

As a Sears Executive, I would get five vacation weeks every year. At first, I let them accumulate until Sears adopted a new policy requiring employees to use all of their vacation time in the same year it was earned or lose it. Traveling with Ali was a perfect way to use my vacation. I traveled with Ali to Japan, Munich, Germany, Africa, London, and other places where his boxing schedule took him. Keeping him from eating junk food wasn't easy. A couple of times I had to threaten to quit.

As was the case with many Black entertainers and sports figures, Ali was loved and appreciated more, by all races, in other countries than he was in his own country. Everywhere we went crowds would gather chanting, "Ali! Ali!" We didn't have to pay for anything; drinks, food, everything was on the house.

If I had used that vacation time to travel with Black people of the Civil Rights Movement, my friends and co-workers would have criticized me. "You're using your time to be with "those people?" But with Ali, it was different. Although it is true that many White people resented Ali because of his affiliation with the Nation of Islam, because he had the audacity to call himself the greatest, and because he was Black, others—especially boxing fans—saw Ali as neither Black nor White. He was, in their eyes and in the eyes of my wife Jean and my sons George, Bob and Mike the greatest boxing champion of the world. My White friends would say, "You're traveling with Ali? Wow! You're really a lucky guy!"

After traveling and spending time together, Ali and I became very close friends. All three of my sons, George, Bob and Mike, were thrilled that their Dad knew the heavyweight champion of the world. I arranged for all of them to meet him and he even gave each one of my sons their own personal copy of a beautiful autographed portrait of Ali and Sonny Liston. My friend, Muhammad Ali, recently passed away. It was a great loss to the world and a personal loss for me.

On one occasion, after returning to the states from traveling with Ali, who didn't drink alcohol at all, I was looking forward to going by the rectory and having a beer with Father Clements, who always had plenty in his refrigerator. At the beginning of our friendship, he would say, "Can I get you a beer, George?" And I'd say, "Yes, thank you, Father." He'd go to the refrigerator and bring me a beer. After awhile, he'd just say, "Help yourself to a beer, George." I knew just where he kept them in the fridge. Pretty soon, he stopped even telling me to help myself; I'd just go to the refrigerator and get a beer, which is exactly what I did when I visited Father at the rectory on that particular day.

To my surprise, there was not one single bottle or can of beer anywhere in the refrigerator. I panicked.

"Father Clements, where's the beer?" I asked.

"I'm not keeping any beer or alcohol here now that my son, Joseph is living in Holy Angels Rectory with me," Father explained.

Father Clements had started a program called One Church One Child to encourage African American parents to adopt African American orphans. He decided to practice what he preached by adopting nine-year-old Joey. I felt very honored and humbled when he asked me to be Joey's godfather. I thought the idea of a priest adopting a child would make a great news story, and when I told my friend, Irv Kupcinet about "One Church One Child" and Father Clements's new son, Joseph, Kup agreed and ran the story in the next day's edition of the *Chicago Sun-Times*. Newspapers throughout the nation and the world picked up the story of the Black Roman Catholic Priest adopting a child.

There was one slight problem. Father Clements had not spoken with Cardinal Cody who, as the head of the Chicago archdiocese, was Father's superior. Naturally, Cardinal Cody was furious that he had to learn about something as important as a priest in his Archdiocese adopting a child through a newspaper article. He immediately called Father Clements to his office.

"You took a vow of celibacy!" he screamed at Father Clements, "How can you have a child?"

Father Clements calmly explained that celibacy had nothing to do with adoption, but Cody refused to hear that. He demanded Father Clements give up the whole idea of adoption and forget about the "One Church One Child" notion.

I'd never seen Father Clements look so sad and depressed as he did when he returned to the rectory after meeting with Cardinal Cody. I begged him not to give up on "One Church One Child," and at the same time, I understood his dilemma. He had no choice. Cody was the Cardinal and to go against his orders qualified as the kind of sin my grandmother might have slipped over into the "mortal sin" column.

Before Father Clements could tell Joseph he couldn't adopt him, the telephone rang, and I answered it. The call came from Rome, Italy. On the other end was a representative from the Vatican. I gave the phone to Father Clements and watched his eyes light up as the caller said,

"The Holy Father is very pleased with what you are doing."

"Did you tell the Cardinal that?" Father Clements asked.

"Oh, yes," the caller replied. "The Holy Father is going to call him next."

About ten minutes later, the phone rang, and again I answered. It was the Archdiocese calling for Father Clements. I gave the phone to Father and watched him as he spoke to the Cardinal and said, "Oh, thank you! Thank you!" One Church One Child had been sanctioned by the Vatican and approved by Cardinal Cody. Father Clements went on to adopt three more boys, Friday, Stewart, and St. Anthony. I became Friday's godfather also.

Today, there are One-Church-One-Child programs in cities across the nation. Father Clements' challenges related to the program inspired the Made-For-TV Movie entitled *The Father Clements Story*. Lou Gossett played Father Clements, Malcolm Jamal Warner portrayed Father Clements' first adopted son, Joey, Carroll O'Connor portrayed Cardinal Cody, and Ron McClarty portrayed me.

CHAPTER 17

Chicago's First Black Mayor

"I want to be a mayor who helped, really helped."
–MAYOR HAROLD WASHINGTON

It seemed like just yesterday that my Grandma was saying, "Those people are nice, as long as they stay in their place." I'd like to say to her well, Grandma, one of "those people" just happened to be the Mayor of the whole city of Chicago so in other words—Chicago was his place."

An extremely intelligent and prolific Congressman by the name of Harold Washington had stolen the hearts of many of the citizens of Chicago, especially those from the Black community. Harold Washington was one of the most personable, genuine human beings I had ever known.

I met Harold long before he began to run for Mayor, although I don't remember exactly how we met. He lived in Hyde Park and I was frequently in that area. Sometimes I'd walk down 55th Street in Hyde Park, and a limo would pull up beside me. The next thing I'd know a window would roll down and I'd hear this big, booming voice say, "George O'Hare! How are you?" There would be Congressman Harold Washington in the limo, all smiles. Sometimes I'd say, "Hey Congressman Washington, how are you?" Other times I'd just say, "Hi Harold!" He never seemed to mind people calling him Harold, even after he became mayor.

I wasn't the only one who was impressed with Congressman Washington. There were many others, including the great African American journalist and community activist, Lu Palmer. Lu Palmer had a daily five-minute radio show sponsored by Illinois Bell. In those five minutes, he would expound on current events affecting African Americans. He would always end the show by saying, "That's enough to make a Negro turn Black." He also expressed his views through his local Chicago newspaper, The *Black X-Press*. Lu and his wife, Jorja English Palmer, were two of the most vocal, hard-working and dedicated community activists in Chicago – and possibly in the Nation.

In 1982, the community was gearing up for another mayoral election. Four years prior, Mayor Jane Byrne had become mayor by unseating Mayor Bilandic. Everyone was upset with Mayor Bilandic's administration's unpreparedness during Chicago's biggest snowstorm. That snowstorm became Jane Byrne's focal point, and the citizens of Chicago rallied around her.

The Black community had held out hope for Mayor Jane Byrne, but to many activists, especially Lu Palmer, Mayor Byrne was a big disappointment. Now Lu and many others felt it was time for the city to elect a Black mayor.

I attended the meetings chaired by Lu Palmer on Chicago's South Side, where discussions were held about who should be drafted to run for Chicago's first Black mayor. I think most of us knew Congressman Washington was the number one choice. He was charismatic, politically astute, and an ideal candidate all around; and having run for Mayor in 1977, he knew the game. Other candidates were considered, including Alderman Anna Langford and Senator Richard Newhouse, but there was no doubt who the chosen one would be when all was said and done. For one thing, while these discussions were going on, a citywide media campaign urging African Americans to "Come Alive, October 5," was also taking place specifically for Harold. He told those who were trying to persuade him to run for Mayor that he would only do so if there were at least 50,000 newly registered African American voters and an initial war chest of a minimum of $250,000.

When Harold announced he was running for Mayor, he chose Renault Robinson as his campaign manager. Former Mayor Daley's son, States Attorney Richard M. Daley, also threw his hat in the ring, which split the White vote between Daley and the incumbent Mayor Jane Byrne, allowing Harold Washington to become the Democratic nominee with thirty-six percent of the vote.

Edward Gardner, the owner of Soft Sheen Products, a very successful Black hair care company, put up money for the voter registration campaign, and subsequently for Harold's campaign. Edwin C. "Bill" Berry, the past Executive Director of the Chicago Urban League, also got involved and brought into the campaign a super activist by the name of Al Raby, who became the Campaign Manager.

When Harold won the primary election, White Democrats who didn't even know they were racists left the party and jumped over to the Republican Party to support the GOP nominee, Bernard Epton. It became widely known throughout the city that Mr. Epton had a lot of problems and had been a guest at Tinley Park's Mental Institution on more than one occasion. Rather than have a Black man as the mayor of the City, people were willing to vote for a mentally challenged person as long as he was White.

On election night, after Epton found out he had lost, he was said to have suffered a nervous breakdown on the elevator. He was readmitted to Tinley Park Mental Institution that night.

Mayor Harold Washington turned out to be one of the best mayors Chicago ever had. Unlike previous Mayors Kelly, Kennelly, and Daley, he wasn't White or Irish Catholic. And in spite of my Uncle Lou's beliefs, I know for a fact Mayor Harold Washington didn't wish to be White—he was proud to be Black.

As gung-ho as I was about working in the Black community, my enthusiasm wasn't shared by my sons, especially my oldest son, George. He would listen just as long as I raved about how wonderful it was for Chicago to have a Black mayor, until he finally got tired of hearing it and would say, "Dad, you already talked about that. I don't want to hear it over and over again." Well, God has a way of putting things in perspective. George was in a leadership position with one of the largest retail liquor establishments in Chicago. They were not too large, however, for the Chicago City Council to give them problems about their liquor license. "Do you think Mayor Washington can help?" he asked me one day. Did I think? I had no doubt the Mayor would find a way to help. I phoned Mayor Washington, and he said what I thought he would say, "Of course I'll meet with your son, George. Bring him down to City Hall."

Despite his busy schedule, Mayor Washington met with George and me for over a half-hour; and even took a picture with us. Before we left his office, Mayor Washington assured George he would look into the situation. Ultimately, he did a lot more than merely look into the situation: he fixed the problem. After that meeting, I could see a difference in George's attitude. He even bragged to his friends that he knew the Mayor of Chicago.

That wasn't the only time one of "those people" came to my son's rescue. When his employers decided they wanted to be known as an equal employment opportunity company, Reverend Jesse Jackson and Willie Barrow helped George to identify at least a dozen African Americans who were ready, willing and able to work in the liquor business. Was George pleased? I'll say he was! In fact, he came to me a little later and said, "Dad, the Black employees you helped us hire are great. Could you see if Reverend Jackson and Reverend Barrow would help us get some more?"

CHAPTER 18

Things White Racists Never Learned

"Prejudice is a great time-saver.
You can form opinions without having to get the facts."
–E. B. WHITE

The phone rang early one Thursday morning. By the time I reached it, the caller had hung up. Seconds later it started ringing again. That time I promptly answered and was greeted by the voice of Reverend Willie Barrow, informing me that Reverend Jackson was calling a staff meeting, and wanted me to be in attendance.

I looked at my watch. It was seven thirty in the morning. I had time to go by the PUSH Offices and still make it to work. Fortunately, I didn't have any meetings at Sears scheduled for that morning.

"I'll be right there," I said, scarfing down a piece of toast and gulping a sip of coffee.

"It's not at PUSH headquarters," Reverend Barrow said.

"Oh, is it going to be held at a church?"

"No, it's going to be at Michael Reese Hospital."

When I got to Michael Reese Hospital, Reverend Jackson was lying there in his hospital gown, surrounded by staff and volunteers. The bed was cluttered with newspapers, just like his bed at home. Reverend Jesse Jackson was a living, breathing idea machine, always thinking of a new project and the fact that he was in the hospital with a bout of pneumonia didn't stop him from working. "We're going to have a Black Expo," he announced. Everyone nodded as if they knew exactly what a Black Expo was. I didn't have any idea what it was, and I wasn't afraid to ask.

"What's a Black Expo?" I asked.

Reverend Jackson didn't mind the question. In fact, he seemed to welcome it.

"Well you see, George, there are a lot of local African American businesses in the community, but most people don't know they exist because they don't have a way to advertise or showcase their products or services."

I listened intently, as did most of his staff and volunteers. I think they were glad I asked the question also.

"So the Black Expo exposes the businesses to the community?" I offered.

"George, you're a smart man," Jesse said, "Yes, the idea of an Expo is to bring the vendors together in one place to expose their goods and services to the public."

Now that everyone had a clear understanding of the meaning of a Black Expo, Jesse began giving out assignments.

"We need to get in touch with some entertainers, Sylvia, call Aretha Franklin and see if you can get a hold of Stevie Wonder."

"What about seminars?" someone asked.

Reverend Jackson thought that was a good idea. "We'll rent booths and tables at a small cost, to African American business owners, retail shop owners, and entrepreneurs so they can display and demonstrate their products and services," he said. He turned to me. "George, I want you to call Kup and your other media contacts and get the word out to all the newspapers."

I was on it. "When is this going to take place?" I asked.

"Oh, we've got plenty of time," said Jesse. "We don't plan to have it until the week after next."

I got the word out to the papers. Jesse was out of the hospital on Saturday, and he announced it at the weekly PUSH Meeting, which broadcasted on WGN-TV and WVON Radio.

The publicity turned out to be extremely impactful. Even in that short period, we managed to fill the International Amphitheater to capacity. The very first PUSH Black Expo was indeed an overwhelming success!

The following year, Operation PUSH was preparing to host its second Black Expo and this time we started earlier. I felt good about what I was doing, volunteering with Operation PUSH and the Movement in general. No longer an outsider, I was accepted; I was a part of the Black community. It had been years since I had even thought about using the n-word. These were my friends. I decided my Uncle Lou was wrong. African Americans were decent people. Many of them were brilliant. All of them were friendly. Ron "Moose" Orr was still my best friend, but now I had two more best friends: Dick Gregory and Father George Clements.

The theme for the second Black Expo was "Save the Children." Once again Jesse invited Black businesses and corporations, such as Johnson Publications (publishers of *Ebony* and *Jet* Magazine) and Johnson Products Company (the largest African American hair care company in the nation) to set up vendor booths. Unlike the previous year's Expo that only showcased businesses and sold goods and services, the second Black Expo also offered employment opportunities.

Many of the celebrity contacts I had acquired through Sears agreed to perform at the five-day exposition. The entertainment line-up included the Staple Singers, the Chi-Lites, Ramsey Lewis, James Cleveland, Isaac Hayes and many others. Every personality that agreed to participate in the Expo was not necessarily a singer, there were also actors and other artists including Richard Roundtree, Ossie Davis and of course, Dick Gregory. The plans were laid out. This Expo was going to be great. Jesse kept thinking, and the ideas kept flowing.

"George, we're going to have a booth on Black inventors at Expo. Do you think you could get Sears to be the sponsor?"

I stood there, dumbfounded. Black inventors? Don't get me wrong; I knew there were Black musicians, Black comedians, Black football, basketball and baseball players, but I also knew for a fact that no Black person had ever invented anything, except maybe peanut butter. If I knew there was no such thing as a Black inventor, as brilliant as Jesse Jackson was, I was sure he must have known that also.

"I can't do that, Jesse," I said.

"Of course you can, George. The top people at Sears love you."

"It's a matter of credibility."

"Credibility? What are you talking about?"

"Upper management puts a lot of trust in me, Jesse. If I go to them with false claims about Black people inventing anything, my credibility goes out of the window."

Jesse looked at me, dumbfounded. "Everybody knows there were Black inventors," he insisted.

I was beginning to get concerned. If Jesse was saying that to make the Black community feel proud, I could understand that; but if he actually believed it, which is what seemed to be the case, well, that appeared to me to be a real problem. I knew White people were fed lies throughout our lives, like Black people had tails and no brains and they all carried razors. But it had never occurred to me that Black people were being fed lies also. I thought to myself that if Jesse had lived all these years with the lie that Black people were inventors, there was nothing I could say to make him see the truth. But I tried to reason with him anyway.

"Jesse, we all know that during slavery, Black people couldn't read or write, so how could they have invented anything?" I asked. Jesse was quiet, so I continued, "I can't go to Sears and talk about Black inventors. They know I volunteer in the Black community, but I can't just make stuff up that isn't true. That would not only hurt my credibility with them, but it would also take away some of the respect they have for you right now."

Jesse was silent. He looked at me for a long time as if he was seeing me for the first time. Then he called his secretary who was in the outer office. In a matter of seconds, she appeared at the door.

"Yes, Reverend?" she said, notebook in hand, pen poised, ready to take instructions.

"Call Mrs. Jackson, and tell her to come down here."

"Yes, Reverend," she repeated and then disappeared back into the outer office.

I didn't know if Jesse's continued silence was a sign of dismissal or not. I rose to go. "Sit down George, my wife will be here in a minute," Jesse said. So I sat and watched Jesse continue with his phone calls and mail, once in awhile calling in a staff member about something that was in the paper or a letter he received. After what seemed like hours, but was no more than twenty minutes, Jesse's beautiful, petite, fashionably dressed wife, Jacqueline Jackson, appeared.

"George here doesn't believe Black people invented anything," Jesse said. "I think he needs an education, so why don't you take him by Doc's?"

Mrs. Jackson smiled and motioned for me to come with her.

The "Doc" Jesse referred to turned out to be a prominent doctor in the Black community. "Doc, Reverend wants George to learn about Black inventors." Jacqueline always referred to her husband as "Reverend" in the presence of friends, associates, and staff. Doc took us down into his basement. Like a museum curator giving me a tour, he provided a little bit of history about each one of the Black inventors depicted in the pictures and posters in his basement.

I paused in front of a picture of a distinguished-looking Black man with a broad mustache and beard wearing what looked like a priest's collar, although I knew he wasn't a priest. The placard beneath his picture read, "Daniel Hale Williams performed the first successful open-heart surgery." That stopped me in my tracks. The first open heart surgery? A Black man did that? Next to Dr. Williams' photo was a picture of Charles Drew. The caption said he was responsible for blood plasma and the blood banks. "He died because he was in an automobile accident," Doc explained, "and the "Whites only" hospital wouldn't admit him so he could receive life-saving blood plasma." I thought of a poster I had seen somewhere that said "Racism Kills!" I wondered how many White lives did Charles Drew's blood plasma save, and yet racism killed him by depriving him of access to his own invention.

I continued to be amazed as I walked around that basement reading about the accomplishments of Black inventors. Garrett Morgan invented the traffic light, another Black person invented the third rail of the trolley, and Black inventors were responsible for bicycle frames, the shoe last, the baby buggy, refrigeration on trucks and so much more. And to think, all my life I was taught that Black people had no brains. The only inventor we learned about in school was Eli Whitney who invented the cotton gin. We could have lived all of our lives without the cotton gin. But open-heart surgery? Blood plasma? The traffic signal? The gas mask? Cortisone? All of these and more were crucial to our very existence, and they were all invented or discovered by Black people. I thought of the many unenlightened individuals who continued to believe the color of a person's skin had anything to do with what's inside of them. I thought of my own ignorance. A few hours before that, I was so sure Black people could not be inventors of anything; yet if God created all men and women equal, then anybody, Black or White, had the capacity to be innovative and creative.

I was hungry for more knowledge about Black inventors. Doc had a couple of small books and one large book about Black inventors. After I had promised to return them in a day or so, he let me borrow them.

By the time I left the doctor's home, it was almost noon. I prided myself on never being late for work, and when I was, no one questioned me. It was nearly 12:30 PM when I arrived at Sears, and I went straight to Mr. Metcalf's office to ask if I could have about thirty minutes of his and other top management's time for a brief meeting. I briefly explained that I wanted to meet about Sears' sponsorship of this year's Black Expo. Mr. Metcalfe agreed. "But no more than thirty minutes." I didn't mention the part about Black inventors which would have entailed another conversation, and I'm sure Mr. Metcalfe wouldn't have agreed so quickly to a meeting.

Once the managers took their seats, Mr. Metcalfe started the meeting. "As you all know," he said, "George has been working with Reverend Jesse Jackson and his Operation Breadbasket or PUSH, or is it now called the Rainbow PUSH Coalition, George?"

"It's both," I said, not wanting to get into a long, drawn-out explanation about Operation PUSH versus the Rainbow PUSH Coalition. But that was my opening, so I went on to explain that Reverend Jesse Jackson had a very successful Black Expo last year and he was going to do it again this year. We talked for another ten or fifteen minutes about Black Expo. Some of the managers had merchandise at the Expo that went very well. Black entertainers were present, and we sold their 45-RPM records and their albums.

"Well, we have another opportunity for more of that great exposure this year," I said, "Reverend Jesse Jackson wants to give Sears a chance to sponsor its Black Inventors booth."

There was complete silence for a full five minutes. Finally one of the managers said,

"What is a Black Inventors booth?"

"I know," another one quipped, "A booth that will feature the guy, what's his name? The one with the peanuts?"

"Black people invented peanuts?"

"Naw, I think it was peanut butter."

"What else?"

"Nothing. Come on, George; you're pulling our legs. You know the Negroes never invented anything."

This discussion went on for quite awhile. I knew my words alone wouldn't convince them, so I reached into my briefcase and took out the books I had borrowed from Doc along with a couple of posters he had given me. I showed them to Mr. Metcalf and the Sears managers.

They read the books in silence, shaking their heads, not wanting to believe, but here it was in black and white in copyrighted books published in the United States. They sat there, speechless. Mr. Metcalf broke the silence. "Tell Reverend Jackson we'd be honored to sponsor the Black Inventor's Booth. The public needs to be made aware of these great inventors and the contributions they made to the nation and the world," The other Sears managers nodded in agreement.

The following week, Sears won the Black Expo contest for having the best booth.

That Black Inventors' booth meant more to me than a great design or an award. It anchored me in my belief that all men are created equal. It was as if a giant eraser had come into my life and erased all the misinformation, the stereotypes, and myths, and opened my eyes to the capabilities and accomplishments of these people whom I once referred to as "those people."

I went to the public library in my White suburban community and asked the librarian for books about Negro inventors. The librarian looked at me as if I had just asked her for books about aliens from space. She gave me a half-smile, half-smirk as if to say, "I'll look it up but there's nothing there." She pulled open a desk drawer and began thumbing through a card catalogue. Her eyes got bigger and bigger as she pulled out card after card, then wrote the titles down and directed me to the shelves where they were located. The books about Negro inventors were in pristine condition; they had clearly never been used.

Nothing keeps racism alive like ignorance. I was brought up to believe that Black people had no brains, no ambition, and no mental skills. Too many Black and White American youth have not learned about the great Black inventors or the many contributions Black people have made to this country and the world. Thus, White people continue to be racists, and Black people continue to have self-hate. Learning about the many accomplishments and contributions of Black people was a huge step toward my recovery from racism.

The Chicago Junior Chamber of Commerce, known as the Jaycees, brought many people into my life whom I would never have met, especially "Father Charles "Dismas" Clark, depicted in a movie as "the Hoodlum Priest."

Dr. Martin Luther King awakened me to the fact that Black people can be articulate and knowledgeable. He introduced me to the Reverend Jesse Jackson, Sr. and through Jesse I learned Black people are far from lazy as I watched him working tirelessly around the clock, with a head full of remarkable concepts and ideas.

Through Dr. King, Jesse Jackson, and Father "Dismas" Clark, I learned to respect Black people.

Fred Hampton and Renault Robinson opened my eyes to the injustices of our so-called justice system and the prejudice, bigotry, and racism practiced against a race of people by police, the very ones who have been called to serve and protect every community and every citizen.

Through " the Greatest" Muhammad Ali; radio celebrity Daddy-O (Holmes) Daylie; Comedian Godfrey Cambridge, George Jones, Vice President of the Joe

Louis Milk Company, and many others, I learned to be comfortable with Black men and women and in Black neighborhoods.

Through my drinking buddy, Don Cornelius, I discovered that Black people dream, too, and they are passionate about making their dreams come true.

Through the Honorable Minister Louis Farrakhan, I learned Catholics are not the only people in the world; there are other religions such as the Nation of Islam, whose members are more committed and more disciplined than most.

Through Lincoln Perry, I learned "Stepin Fetchit" is no name for a dog because it's the name of one of the greatest entertainers and human beings I've ever been honored to meet.

Harold Washington showed me that a Black person could be smart enough, charismatic enough and politically astute enough to become Mayor of the second largest city in the world.

And through two of the greatest people I've ever met, my mentors, role models, and best friends, Dick Gregory and Father George Clements, I discovered that it is possible to love, I mean really love, someone whose skin is a different color.

There is a song that goes, "To know, know, know you; is to love, love, love you." I know them, and I love them, and I'm very proud to be called "nigger-lover" by a group of older, misguided and misinformed White American people.

In spite of all I learned from my friends and mentors in the Black community, I learned so much more in Doc's basement, and from the award-winning Black Inventor's booth at PUSH'S Black Expo. Those revelations, along with my further research at the public library, wiped away the negative propaganda about Black people I had been inundated with all my life and brought me closer to recovery from my racism. My mind was no longer encumbered with the falsehoods I was taught growing up. With an open and enlightened mind, I felt I was free to love my Black brothers and sisters with the brotherly love Christ told us to extend to each other. I understood what Rev. Dr. Martin Luther King, Jr. meant and what he must have been feeling when he said, "Free at Last, Free at Last, Thank God Almighty I'm free at last!"

CHAPTER 19

Life after Sears

"Choose a work that you love and you won't have to work another day.
—CONFUCIUS

By 1984, race relations in Chicago appeared to be much better, at least on the surface. Mayor Washington continued to get opposition from his City Council, with twenty-nine Council members siding with his nemesis, Alderman Ed Vrydolyak, versus the twenty-one council members in Mayor Washington's corner. Good things happened for Chicago, too. Job opportunities grew, and crime decreased. According to the rumor mill, the so-called Black gang leaders didn't want to embarrass the first Black mayor by committing crimes on his watch.

At fifty-eight years old, I was ready to start on a whole new path. I had given thirty-four years of my life to Sears, Roebuck and Company, and I knew it was time to move on for several reasons.

173

For one thing, the Sears I loved had changed so much I hardly recognized it. The new person heading up the company had made his fortune in the insurance and real estate businesses, so in my opinion, he treated Sears as if it was just another money-making commodity instead of a group of up and coming young men and women whose mission was to change the world for the better.

There were four more important reasons for my early retirement; one wonderful woman by the name of Jean O'Hare, and three great sons, George O'Hare III, Robert O'Hare, and Michael O'Hare. I wanted to give them back some of the time I had spent working and traveling for Sears, as well as marching, meeting, and volunteering for the Civil Rights of the African American people.

My primary reason for retirement had to do with a career change I had in mind. Having discovered the joy of motivational speaking, I decided to dedicate the remainder of my life to my family and motivational speaking.

I learned the art and fundamentals of motivational speaking from many sources, including My Uncle "Husk" O'Hare, Dale Carnegie, Zig Ziglar, and Norman Vincent Peale. I watched these people, studied them, and took all of their good points to heart. Perhaps the most valuable lesson my Uncle Husk gave me was to always "accentuate the positive." At that time I realized within my thirty-four years at Sears, I had transitioned from being obsessed with the lonely sport of swimming to meeting customers as a salesman and sales manager and, ultimately, having a passion for speaking to hundreds of people, especially the youth.

Don't get me wrong; I still love swimming to this day, but I am so much more excited about having the opportunity to tell the world "A smile is worth a million dollars and it doesn't cost a penny. Laugh and the world laughs with you, cry, and you cry alone."

I had a lifetime of experiences I wanted to share. I wanted all children, regardless of the color of their skin, to know how important they are and to learn that they have a tremendous future ahead of them in this great world and marvelous country. I wanted to be one of the voices that inspired them to go after their dreams. I wanted all people, young and old, to know the greatest gift is "love" and God commanded us to love each other, regardless of our differences, because we are all His children.

At Sears, I was sharing my knowledge with the salesmen and sales managers, not only telling them the techniques of selling but also motivating them to be the best they could be—and I loved it! As my love for being a salesman dwindled, my love for motivational speaking soared!

So at two years shy of sixty, I retired from Sears, Roebuck and Company to pursue that new and exciting life. I was doing what I loved and spending more time with my family. I was happy, and the family was happy about my decision. In fact, the only person who was most unhappy about me leaving Sears was my friend, Don Cornelius.

When I got the call from Don, I thought he was going to congratulate me; instead, he angrily attacked me. "George, what are you doing?" he said, "You can't quit Sears! You can't retire!" Later I mentioned his outburst to Dick Gregory, who said, "Of course Don Cornelius would be upset. You're sponsoring his show. How else could a Black guy get on worldwide TV with a Soul Train?" I still couldn't understand why Don was so upset. The show was still on the air at that time, and it was doing great.

Rather than worry about who was upset about my leaving Sears, I focused my energy toward becoming the best motivational speaker I could be. I began to not only listen to the greats but also to study their techniques. I'd read the newspapers every day, not only to keep abreast of the news, but also to find out who was speaking where, and if they sounded interesting I would go to see them, no matter how famous or obscure they were. If it meant traveling out of town to hear Dr.Norman Vincent Peale, Dale Carnegie or Zig Ziglar, I'd go.

People who don't go to hear motivational speakers or who don't at least listen to their tapes are missing out on some life-changing experiences.

I am an eyewitness to the way Dale Carnegie changed my youngest son, Michael. Concerned that he was too quiet and too shy (like I was at his age) I paid $450 to sign him up for a Dale Carnegie course. After I signing him up, I told him he didn't have to take the course if he felt uncomfortable, but Michael gladly went, and we were both happy with the outcome. Michael emerged from the class as a brand new person. If you met this friendly, uplifting, good-natured, and gregarious young man today, you would never believe he was once bashful and quiet. That one Dale Carnegie course changed his life.

At times, I felt like I was back in a classroom and my teachers were Zig Ziglar, Norman Vincent Peale, Dale Carnegie, and Les Brown. When I wasn't attending one of their seminars or listening to their tapes, I was volunteering to speak to employees or sales staff of a corporation. I learned that sometimes you have to give away your services to be recognized. Occasionally I'd just ask company managers if they had sales meetings and if they said yes, I'd tell them that I'd like to come and observe because I'm writing an article about sales techniques. I'd sit in the back and ask them not to tell the sales team my purpose for being there. Then, I would watch and listen and determine what they needed. I'd be back a week or so later with a proposal. That tactic worked. Pretty soon I was being asked to speak almost everywhere, and I was making good money doing it.

What I wanted more than anything was to reach young people. It's my opinion the public school system tries to teach their students how to make a living, but I want to teach them how to live successfully with a positive attitude and positive thinking.

Before Harold Washington became Chicago's mayor, his predecessor, Mayor Jane Byrne, had gifted the Chicago Public School System with an incredible, capable woman by the name of Ruth Love. Ruth Love was the first female and the first African-American Superintendent of Chicago Public Schools. She did a great job with the schools in Oakland, California, and she was already doing tremendous things for the Chicago Public Schools.

Dick Gregory invited me to dinner where he introduced me to Dr. Ruth Love. During dinner, he told Dr. Love I was a motivational speaker. Then he said something I totally did not expect, "I want you to book my friend George O'Hare to speak at every non-academy and non-magnet school in the Chicago Public School system every day, with the understanding that when he has a paying gig he can re-schedule his speaking engagement with the school."

Gregory's rationale was that academies and charter schools had everything they needed to give kids a quality education, but the public schools, where mostly poor kids attended, were the ones needing help. Dr. Love agreed, and let me tell you, it was great!

Repetition is the mother of all learning, and by helping to provide me with speaking engagements, even though they were pro-bono, Dick Gregory was giving me the exposure, practice, and experience I needed to become a great motivational speaker. I loved talking to the little kids, and I learned that the fourth, fifth, sixth and seventh graders were the ones that appreciated my speeches the most.

Although I spoke to the public school children pro-bono, when I was requested to speak to teachers, principals or administrators, I always received a fee.

I was overwhelmed by Dick Gregory's friendship and loyalty. Here he was, a super great comedian and probably ten times busier than me, yet he took the time to talk to Dr. Ruth Love about having me speak at the schools to get the experience I needed to become a seasoned motivational speaker.

Gregory also took an interest in me in other ways. One day I was going to speak to a small community group and knowing the attendees would probably be dressed casually, I dressed casually also. It just so happened that Dick Gregory was in town, and he stopped by as I was preparing to leave.

"Where you going?" he asked.

I told him I was going to speak to a group.

"Dressed like that?" he said.

"Sure," I said. "What's wrong with the way I'm dressed?"

He told me if he came into a room to speak everyone knew who he was, but if I came to give a speech, the people would say, "Who is he?"

"So, since they don't know you," he said, "You've got to dress like you're important—navy blue suit, red tie, red pocket handkerchief and white shirt."

His little lecture reminded me of what my Grandma often said, "A first impression is a lasting impression. Always dress to impress." I took Grandma's and Dick Gregory's advice and from that time until today; I don't go out of the house unless I'm wearing my "uniform" --navy blue suit, red tie, red pocket handkerchief and white shirt.

During that time, Illinois was fortunate enough to have who I think was one of the greatest Attorney Generals ever, Neil Hartigan. He spoke out against many of the evils taking place in the corporate and political arena. He felt it was time for America to change her ways—her racist, war-mongering, greedy ways—and he wouldn't have minded at all if that change started in Illinois.

The first time I met Attorney General Hartigan was at a State of Illinois event, where we were both speakers. After I had spoken, he approached me and said, "I was very impressed with your speech and would like you to be part of my staff." I thanked him, and he gave me his card. "Give me a call next week," he said. Well, I didn't call him, but I saw him about a month later at a luncheon. "You didn't call me." He said. I apologized, although I purposely hadn't called because I had no desire to work on his or anyone's staff. He accepted my apology and we agreed to meet at his office the next day.

At that meeting, he repeated his initial offer,

"I want you to be part of my staff, and I can only pay you a stipend of fifty thousand dollars a year."

I told him I had retired to do what I wanted to do and to spend more time with my family. "I can't give you one hundred percent of my day," I explained.

Attorney General Hartigan laughed and said, "I'm not offering you a job with benefits. The price I would pay would be a stipend for you to come and speak to the senior citizens of Illinois every three months."

Well, that sounded pretty good, so I took it, and for seven years I was part of Attorney General Neil Hartigan's team, attending senior events, speaking to the elderly and agencies for the aged, and advocating for older adults throughout the State of Illinois.

One day, after speaking to a group of students at Kennedy-King Community College, I saw my friend, Hermene Hartman, who was an educator at the college. Hermene introduced me to Dr. Salvatore Rotella, the Chancellor of the Chicago City Colleges.

"And what do you do, Mr. O'Hare?" Dr. Rotella asked.

"I'm a motivational speaker," I explained.

"How much do you charge?" he wanted to know.

I told him I charged whatever a person securing my services could afford and for people who don't have any money, "I volunteer," I said laughingly. He hired me to speak to the City Colleges for one thousand dollars per speech.

"You're doing a great job, George," Hermene said to me one day.

"All I do is accentuate the positive," I told her. Then I playfully began to sing Johnny Mercer's song, "You've got to ac-cent-uate the positive, e-lim-inate the negative, latch on to the affirmative, and don't mess with Mr. In-Between."

I could almost see a light bulb go off in her head. "Accentuate the positive," she repeated. She then said, "George, I've got a great idea! You're going on television." "I am? That's great!" I said. And that was the beginning of my radio and television program, "Accentuate the Positive."

The show featured interviews with popular celebrity role models, newspaper people, sports personalities, educators, and businessmen and women. We interviewed religious and civic leaders, authors, judges, lawyers, and health and nutrition experts and hundreds of notables from all walks of life. Of course, I interviewed Dick Gregory, Father George Clements, and the late, great Reverend Willie Taplin Barrow. Others included Channel five news anchor Warner Saunders, who became my very dear friend and confidant; Marva Collins, a brilliant woman who had an idea of how to successfully educate children, and it worked; and Roland Burris, another good friend who was also the first African-American Illinois Comptroller and Illinois Attorney General. He would have been the second Black Federal Senator from Illinois (Carol Mosely Braun was the first) if politics hadn't gotten in the way of putting a qualified man in the office to which he belonged.

Among my favorite interviewees was Edward Gardner, one of the first Black leaders and the founder and owner of Soft Sheen Products Company in Chicago. Ed Gardner had raised and put the money up for the "Come Alive, October 5," voter registration campaign, resulting in the registration of 200,000 new African American voters. He even raised funds and personally bankrolled Illinois Congressman Harold Washington's historic campaign to become Chicago's first Black Mayor.

I continued my new career as a motivational speaker, and I also continued my quest to be the best I could be by going to see and hear as many great speakers as I could. It didn't matter whether the person was a known motivational speaker, a politician, or someone in the community. Whenever I read about or heard someone was going to be speaking, I'd call and get the details and then make my way to the hall, church, hotel, school or wherever they would be lecturing.

One day I read in the paper that a candidate for Illinois Senate by the name of Barack Obama was speaking at a Protestant Church on Chicago's West Side. I was curious to hear what anyone with such an unusual name would have to say, so I decided to go. When I arrived there was a small crowd of about twenty-five people in the large church, which could have easily held about a thousand. the The size of the church, the number of attendees, the unusual name; all that left my mind as I sat and listened to this very young man give an eloquent and extremely charismatic speech. I was so impressed by that at the conclusion of his speech, I walked up to the pulpit and placed one hundred dollars in his hand.

Before I went home, I stopped by Holy Angels Catholic Church Rectory. I was excited about what I heard and wanted to share it with Father Clements. "I just heard this young man speak and he was really great," I said. I told Father Clements about the speech and how I was moved to give the young man a hundred dollars.

"What's his name?" Father Clements wanted to know.

When I told him it was Barack Obama, he said. "Oh, he's speaking at Hales Franciscan High School tomorrow."

"Great!" I said, "I'd like to hear him again."

The next afternoon, when Father Clements and I arrived at Hales Franciscan High School, the program had already started although Barack Obama hadn't arrived yet. The large gymnasium was almost full, and Father Clements and I made our way to the middle of the gymnasium where we found a couple of seats. A few minutes later, Barack Obama came in and took his place on the stage. He looked out into the audience and suddenly got up from his seat and came down off of the stage, and walked through the crowds of people to the middle section where Father Clements and I were seated. Barack extended his hand to me and said, "I see you're here to see me again." I told him how much I enjoyed his speech the day before and introduced him to Father Clements. Obama thanked me for the one hundred dollars I had given him the previous night and then walked back up to the podium.

I was so impressed with Barack Obama after hearing him speak a second time I told a group of former Sears' employees about him. We had formed our retiree's group after leaving Sears and met about once every three months. I thought this young man would be a great speaker for our group. Based on my word and my enthusiasm, they agreed they would like to hear him speak.

I called everyone who had a number for Barack Obama as I tried to find a way to contact him. My friends were more than willing to help, and everyone who had a number for him gave that number to me. I called every number I was given and left message after message after message. No one called me back. Finally, I just gave up.

A few weeks later, Father Clements and I went to another church where Barack Obama was speaking. The crowds seemed to be getting bigger and bigger. I guess word got around about what a great speaker he was. When he arrived at the church, he went to the pulpit and looked out at the crowd. He abruptly came down from the pulpit and made his way to the pew where Father Clements and I were seated. He shook our hands and then turned to me, smiling sheepishly.

"I think I owe you some phone calls."

"Yes, you do."

"What can I do for you?"

"I'd like you to come and speak to my Sears Retirement group."

"I'd like that."

Barack pointed to a tall, somber-looking man standing on the sidelines. "See that fellow?" he said, "Give him the information, and he'll help make it happen." I gave the man all the details about the retiree group as well as my contact information.

Senator Obama and I never made contact. By that time, his campaign was heating up, and I was sure his schedule was full. I continue to believe he would have accommodated our little group if he had the time.

CHAPTER 20

Association of Recovering Racists

*"Hey White people, if you really want to help end racism
you need to invest in other White people."*
–KAREN HOUSE

B esides going to hear every speaker I learned about, I was also beginning
to have more and more speaking engagements myself; most of which
entailed speaking to corporations and sales staffs. I was still actively going
to schools and volunteering to talk to educators, business leaders, and students
whenever I didn't have a paid engagement. Plus, I was having the time of my life
with my radio and TV interviews. Still, the most pressing thing in my life was to
help in any way I could to make Dr. Martin Luther King's dream a reality—to
help bring about the day when people would not be judged by the color of their
skin but by the content of their character.

I wanted to continue to learn from Black people as well. Therefore, anytime
there was a meeting in the Black community about a Black issue, a political issue

or an organizational issue, I'd be there. I still went to the meetings at Dr. Odom's and George Jones' homes, although the number and frequency of meetings decreased. I still volunteered for Jesse Jackson, and I continued to remain friends with others I had met through Dr. King or Dick Gregory or on my own.

After Dr. King's death, Jesse renamed Operation Breadbasket, Operation PUSH, which at first meant "People United to Save Humanity." Now it's "People United to *Serve* Humanity." I took my three sons George, Bob, and Mike to PUSH meetings with me from the time they were three, five, and seven years of age until they reached their teens and decided they wanted to do something else with their Saturday mornings. I continued attending, not only the Saturday morning PUSH meetings but also the special evening meetings Reverend Jesse Jackson would frequently call.

As I sat in a PUSH meeting one night, a Black woman seated next to me asked, "What are you doing here?" I explained my commitment to the Civil Rights Movement. I told her I believed in equality for all people and wanted to do whatever I could to help the cause." "Then, you don't belong here," she said, "You should go back and talk to your own people." I didn't say anything to that woman for the rest of the meeting, and she didn't say anything else to me, except to glare in my direction every once in awhile. What did she mean "your people?" I wondered. Didn't she understand, just by the fact that I was at the meeting, that I considered Black people my people also?

That incident stayed on my mind, and of course, I told Gregory about what happened as soon as I got the opportunity. His answer surprised me. "She's right," he said, "There are plenty of people talking to the Black community, but who is talking to the racists in the White community?" I guess I never thought about it that way.

I had been living two lives. There was the George O'Hare volunteering for Reverend Jesse Jackson, Father George Clements, and Renault Robinson's African American Police League on the South Side of Chicago, marching with King, committed to the cause. Then there was George O'Hare a typical white, middle-class suburbanite, with racist neighbors and friends. I knew their negative stereotypical concepts of Black people were false, but I seldom corrected them.

Of course, the woman was right, but I couldn't accept what she said until my beloved friend, Dick Gregory, explained in blunt terms exactly what she meant, and on top of that he agreed with her. I'm grateful to have a friend who cared enough about me to tell me the truth.

The words she spoke were like someone putting a mirror up to my face. Here I was, completely knowledgeable about how wrong and sinful racism was; and how wrong the lies and myths that White people had been told throughout their lives about Black people were. I knew the truth, but I was keeping this knowledge to myself instead of sharing it with other misguided White people. In my silence, I was depriving my friends and neighbors of the opportunity to free themselves from their racist thoughts and beliefs.

One of my racist neighbors was a retired ball player. One day he saw me in the yard and came over to do his usual bragging about his professional career and his exceptional skills. The conversation was going well until he began boasting about how he was purposely throwing balls to hit the Black players in the head. "I was "beaning" those damn niggers all summer," he said. He didn't understand my sudden change of mood. I thought about Grandma who would have said, "Don't call them niggers, call them Negroes." I couldn't be pleasant like Grandma. This time I did speak up. I told him I didn't appreciate him using that word to describe a group of people he knew nothing about and who had never done anything to him. He seemed a little surprised. He probably didn't think it would bother me, but it did. After that, the conversation got a little awkward, and he finally left.

When I told Dick Gregory about that incident, I was still fuming. Gregory said exactly what I thought he would say. "You can't worry about those people, George. Just let it roll off your back, smile, and keep on going."

Gregory was doing a lot of traveling during those days, but whenever he was in Chicago, we'd get together. On one such occasion he said, "George, I met a friend of yours on the plane on my way back to Chicago."

"A friend of mine?"

"Yeah, a big White guy was sitting next to me on the plane, and he recognized me and told me his neighbor talked about me all the time. When I asked him who his neighbor was, he said 'George O'Hare.'"

"Did he tell you his name?" I asked.

"He sure did," Greg said, "And when I heard it, it rang a bell, so I asked him what he did for a living, and he said he was a ball player."

"That's the guy I was telling you about," I said.

"Yeah, I know," Greg said, "And you could almost see his ego inflate when I told him I had heard of him."

Now Greg was laughing. "I told him, I'd bet he spent his summer beaning niggers."

Gregory said the former ball player turned a couple of shades of red, lowered his head, and had nothing else to say for the rest of the flight.

I was glad I had told Greg about that guy.

The next time one of my neighbors started talking about "those people" I was ready for them. I would ask them, "Do you believe in God?" "Of course, I believe in God," they would answer. Then I'd say, "And do you think God made everybody—White people, Black people, Brown, Red, and Yellow?"

I could tell they hadn't thought about this much before now. Several seconds would pass before they would slowly say, "Yeah, of course, God made everybody."

"Then why are you arguing with God?" I'd ask them.

They'd get defensive and answer, "I'm not arguing with God,"

"Well if God made everybody, and you have a problem with some of the people He made, then you're telling Him you are doubtful about what He has done."

When I'd say that to them, they'd get quiet, and I knew I had put something serious on their minds.

Sometimes I'd come at them another way. When they started talking about the "niggers weren't any good and had no brains," I'd ask them, "Do you know anyone who has had open heart surgery?"

"Sure, my mother."

"Well, how's your mom doing now?"

"Oh, she's doing just great."

"So a Black man saved your mother's life."

"Naw, a nigger didn't have anything to do with my mother's heart surgery, it was the White doctors in a White hospital."

"But it was a Black man, Daniel Hale Williams, that made medical history by performing the first successful open heart surgery, and every heart surgeon uses his technique today, including the ones that operated on your mother."

The magnitude of this kind of revelation to a White racist is like living all of your life thinking the world is flat and suddenly finding out it's round. Everybody didn't react to this revelation in the same way, but everyone reacted. Some would believe me and also become angry. They didn't want to hear it. Others would say, "I'm going to look that up. I don't believe it's true." There were those who flat out didn't believe Black people were capable of doing anything worthwhile, especially something as complex as open-heart surgery. Their racist minds were made up, and they were not going to allow themselves to be "confused by the facts."

And then there were those who believed it but determined Daniel Hale Williams must have been an exception, the one and only Black person on the planet with a modicum of intelligence. One said to me, "I bet no other nigger did anything worthwhile." That was just the opening I needed.

"Ever hear of Garrett Morgan?"

"No, who's he?"

"He's the Negro who invented the traffic signal and the gas mask." (Stunned silence.)

"Ever hear of Percy Julian?"

Some would respond by saying, "No, look, I've really got to go."

But I would tell them, "He's the Black man that discovered the value of Cortisone and invented the foam used to put out fires."

That revelation resulted in stunned silence accompanied by brewing anger.

Learning that Black people had a history, a culture and were intelligent to boot was a lot for a racist to take in, all in one day. I decided to let this new knowledge brew in their minds for a day or two before I'd tell them about Dr. Shirley Jackson, the Black woman who invented the touch-tone telephone, the portable fax, caller ID, call waiting, and the fiber-optic cable. The truly racist person would probably implode if they were given too much of these truths at one time, so I'd spoon-feed the information to them and give them a little while to digest it. After a week or so, I might tell them about Marie Van Brittan Brown, the Black woman who developed a patent for closed-circuit television security, which is widely used for surveillance, crime prevention, and traffic monitoring. That would take a few days to swallow, so I'd have to wait a little longer to tell them about Esther Okade, the ten-year-old African American math genius who was about to enter college. It was my hope and prayer, that after learning about Thessalonika Arzu-Embry, who earned a Bachelor's Degree in Psychology at the age of fourteen and a Master's in Business Administration at the age of sixteen, their minds would become somewhat open to the fact that Black people are not inherently dumb. One of my racist friends who swore he wasn't a racist, tried to discredit me by looking up Thessalonika Arzu-Embry for himself. His plan backfired. Not only did he learn that she truly exists and everything I said was true, but he also came across a little bit of information I had failed to tell him— the fact that Ms. Arzu-Embry has already written three best-selling books.

Hearing someone say, "George, you're right" was music to my ears. Witnessing a racist evolve into a thoughtful, intelligent human being with a mind that could actually grasp the concept that all men and women are created equal was like a dream come true.

Although I was happy to see some people beginning to open their minds; the problem was the world had far too many racists in it. Talking to two or three of my neighbors wouldn't even make a dent. What was needed was a way to reach a broad range of people, mainly White people, deprived all of their lives of the truth about Black people.

Then an idea hit me, and I told Father Clements. "Father, I'm going to start an 'Association of Recovering Racists.'" "Why recovering and not recovered?" he asked. I reminded him of my Uncle Lou. Even though Uncle Lou had learned the evils of alcohol and never took another drink in his life, he was still not a *recovered* alcoholic; he was a *recovering* alcoholic. If he had ever considered himself recovered, then he would have stopped working at it. "Now, as for me," I said, "As a recovering racist, I have been working hard on my recovery for over forty years. I've been out in the community, I volunteer, I learn. If I ever considered myself completely recovered, then I'd just stop learning, stop volunteering, stop meeting new people, stop talking and stop listening, and go back to my little White suburban home and say 'I'm recovered.'" And most tragic of all, I'd stop asking God to personally help me to learn not only how to eradicate any latent racist views that might be hovering very deep within my spirit, but also to help me reach out to those who need healing from this terrible disease called racism." Of course, Father Clements understood entirely and agreed. I was preaching to the choir, but by doing so, it helped me to find a way to explain the concept of a "recovering racist" to others.

We decided to call the association the "National Association of Recovering Racists for Peace," because racism wasn't just limited to Chicago, it was nationwide. Father Clements pointed out the fact that racists didn't particularly like being called racists, so we developed a sub-division of our organization called "Cultural Diversity for Peace." Our stated mission was (and still is) to eradicate racism starting with self, by using the formulas "Do unto others as you would have them do unto you" and "Forgive us our trespasses as we forgive those who trespass against us."

Putting the Association and the website together was one of the most exciting and fulfilling things I have ever done in my life. I became the founder, president, and CEO of the association. Dick Gregory became the Chairman of the Advisory Board. The advisory board consisted of the late Reverend Willie Taplin Barrow, whom I miss every day; Sister Anita Baird, DHM, the Director of the Office of Racial Justice of the Catholic Archdiocese of Chicago; and of course Father George Clements.

Everybody had input into the final product. When we were creating the letterhead, Father Clements said: "We've got to get St. Francis of Assisi's statement in there somewhere." Everyone agreed. That's why the bottom of our letterhead reads, "*Lord make me an instrument of your peace. Where there is hatred, let me bring love. Where there is doubt, let me instill faith. Where there is darkness, let me bring light. Where there is sadness, let me bring joy. Oh, Divine Master, grant that I may not so much seek to be understood as to understand, to be consoled as to console, to be loved as to love. For it is in giving that we receive, it is in pardoning that we are pardoned, and it is in dying that we are born into everlasting life.*"

The existence of racism in the Catholic Church was officially recognized and deemed a sin in 2000 when two Catholic School students beat Lenard Clark, a Black teenager, into a coma because he had crossed the line from the

Black neighborhood of Bronzeville into the all-White community of Bridgeport, Illinois.

Those young White boys had the same racist upbringing and mindset all of us White lifeguards had back in the day when we were protecting our all White Chicago beaches. Then, we were trying to drown the Black people who would dare set foot on our precious White-folks-only beaches.

But that was back in 1942 when there were no mini-cams or news crews to come to the beaches and record that bigotry. It was different in 2000. The incident was in the news and on the lips of every Chicagoan, Black, White, and Brown. Everybody was watching and waiting to see what the Catholic Church was going to do to address this grievous sin.

Cardinal George responded by establishing the "Archdiocese of Chicago Office of Racial Justice," which had a staff of two: Sister Anita Baird and her assistant, Sister Lois. These two women were remarkable for their commitment and dedication to bring about equality and awareness of the mortal sin of racism, no matter how the perpetrators tried to disguise it. Sister Baird and Sister Lois held one-day Archdiocese anti-racism introductory workshops for employees to help them recognize systemic racism within the workplace. They also held two and a half day training sessions for department directors and school principals, especially those within the Archdiocese of Chicago.

In October 2005, the Office of Racial Justice held a Unity Rally to celebrate the racial and ethnic diversity in the Archdiocese of Chicago. The theme of the rally, dedicated to the Hurricane Katrina survivors, was "Building Bridges and Uniting People." Sister Anita Baird invited Dick Gregory and me to participate in the rally.

October 7, 2005, was surprisingly warm for that time year. Even though this unseasonably warm weather visits us every October, it's still always a pleasant surprise, especially if you're holding an outdoor rally. The Rally took place in River Forest, Illinois. Cardinal Francis George gave an opening prayer; Dick Gregory gave an excellent, moving, humorous, thought-provoking presentation, and the Auxiliary Bishop Joseph N. Perry gave the closing prayer.

I was thrilled by Cardinal George's remarks. In fact, the Catholic *New World* newspaper reprinted a portion of his speech:

"The sin, the crime, the tragedy, the horror of racism is not a good thing to rally around. But it is a good thing to challenge us to take notice. Racism is the original sin of American society, and it will take more than workshops and rallies to overcome it. It has a long history, and it needs a long-range plan—a battle plan, if you will, to address it. It will take all the resources available, including the grace of God, to change people's hearts. The need was made heartbreakingly clear in the wake of Hurricane Katrina when most of the people left stranded were poor and African American." (Excerpted from Racial, Ethnic Groups Build Bridges in Harmony, Catholic New World Newspaper (October 9-22, 2005)

Dick Gregory followed with a dynamic speech that was on point, as usual. He told the crowd that the horrible things that happened in New Orleans as a result of Hurricane Katrina just gave the rest of the world a look at America's racism. In spite of that, Gregory was positive and emphasized that the United States had come a long way.

"Forty years ago, every time I went to Mississippi I knew I'd be killed," he said. "Thank God, I went anyway. Forty years later, the head of the Mississippi state troopers is a Black man. The leader of the Mississippi Department of social services is a Black woman."

Cheers and applause went up at those words. Gregory talked about how Americans keep talking about "Black on Black" crime. "Why aren't they talking about 'White-on-White crime?" he said. He explained that people kill where they live, and too many people don't know that people in every city in the United States are living like the poorer citizens of New Orleans who didn't have a way to get out of the city when the hurricane struck.

I thought about what that woman at the Rainbow PUSH meeting said, "Why don't you go back and talk to your own White people and try to change them?" My own people were White people—especially the White Catholics. With the help of Father Clements, Reverend Willie Taplin Barrow, and others, I immediately produced a DVD along with some printed material telling how Dick Gregory and Father Clements helped me to become a recovering racist. I sent that, along with a copy of the Catholic *New World* newspaper, with its account of the rally, to 300 Bishops, Archbishops, and Cardinals in the United States. I also sent a copy to Pope Benedict XVI. The cover letter came from the "Cultural Diversity …For Peace" a division of the National Association of Recovering Racists, and directed the recipients to our website, www.recoveringracist.com.

Out of three hundred letters, we only received four responses, but I immediately copied those replies and sent them to every Bishop and Cardinal in the country. One letter was from the Vatican, letting me know the Holy Father had received my letter and DVD and also letting me know how much the Pope appreciated the sentiments which prompted me to write him. Dick Gregory told me that I might be one of a very few people in America who had received a message from the Pope. I also received a letter from Cardinal Egan, the Archbishop of New York. Cardinal Egan had been a part of the Civil Rights Movement. He actively engaged in the marches and the rallies, but his carefully worded, politically correct letter did not reflect the commitment I knew he had to equality of the races. Most Reverend Peter A. Rosazza, D.D., the Auxiliary Bishop Episcopal Vicar for the Hispanic Apostolate and the Most Reverend Robert J. Baker, from the Office of the Bishop of Charleston, South Carolina, also sent letters thanking me for the DVDs and for sharing the remarks of Cardinal George and Dick Gregory.

I hoped that seeing these letters, especially Cardinal George's remark that "racism is the original sin of American society," would awaken something in the consciousness of the other White Catholics. Perhaps those who had spent their lives thinking they were doing well and were paving their way to heaven would not only think about mending their ways, but would also preach to their constituencies and congregations the fact that racism is just as serious a sin as any other sin and sin is a barrier to heaven.

CHAPTER 21

Anti-Semitism

"Anti-Semitism has no historical, political, and certainly no philosophical origins. Anti-Semitism is a contagious disease."
–DANIEL BARENBOIM

I don't know if there is a Dr. King-like person who is Jewish and is leading America away from anti-Semitism, but I know even today, anti-Semitism is a huge problem.

Just as I was raised in a racist household and taught to be racist; I was also brought up in an anti-Semitic household and taught to hate Jews. Every day I would sit at the dinner table with my grandmother, grandfather, and Uncle Lou and listen to my Uncle Lou talk about the "Goddamn niggers and Jews." Although my grandmother would always say, "Don't say niggers say Negroes'" she never said anything about the Jewish part of Uncle Lou's rant.

Looking back, I never really understood why we were taught to hate Jews. Did we learn to resent them because they dressed nicer or had more money?

Were they successful in their business life and in most cases better educated, whether they owned businesses or worked successfully for somebody else?

Jewish people survived because they worked together and cared about each other. I remember growing up they had their own Jewish neighborhood and business district on Maxwell Street where everyone would go to get things at lower prices. In those days, we wrongfully called Maxwell Street "Jew Town."

I don't know why this computer inside of my head known as my brain had been programmed by my family, my neighbors, and associates to discriminate against Jewish people. I do know all of that began to change when I was the sales manager at Sears, Roebuck and Company. On one particular day, I received a call from the head of personnel. "George, we have a new employee for you to hire," she said. I told her I was glad. Then after a long pause, she said, "He's Jewish." I didn't say anything, although a dozen thoughts ran through my mind. What would Uncle Lou say about me hiring a Jewish person? Then, as if reading my mind she said, "Sears does not discriminate against Jews, and I hope you would understand and respect that policy and treat him as you would treat anybody else."

The next thing I knew, I was being introduced to the new potential Sears employee who happened to be Jewish. I was in the middle of demonstrating a vacuum cleaner to some customers, and as he watched, the phone rang, and I gestured for him to answer it. "It's for you, Mr. O'Hare," he said. He handed me the phone, and while I engaged in a conversation with one of the managers, this young, Jewish man proceeded to finish my demonstration. By the time I finished that phone conversation, he had sold two vacuum cleaners. Right then and there I began to change my mind regarding Jewish people. Obviously, they have tremendous talent. I hired him that day, and he did a great job for Sears.

I believe the problems of both racism and anti-Semitism continue to exist today. Do the religious institutions actually teach that all mankind—men and women—are created equal? Perhaps there should be an Organization for Recovering Anti-Semitists. Maybe that should be the subject of a future book entitled, "Confessions of a Recovering Anti-Semite (or Jew Hater): Father forgive us!!"

CHAPTER 22

Fake It until You Make It

*Father Clements is my friend and spiritual advisor. Dick Gregory is my
friend and mentor. When I would get exasperated with the racism of other
Whites, Gregory was always quick to tell me to just let it go. "Just smile
and keep on going," he would say. In other words, "fake it until you make
it." That's not always easy to do.*

Looking back on my journey, I know I've come a long way from my racist
beginnings on the West Side of Chicago. As a child, I realized my parents,
grandparents, aunts, and uncle loved me and wanted me to know how
special I was to them. One way of showing me I was special was to denigrate
those people whose skin color was different from mine. I grew up knowing I
could go anywhere at any time and be accepted, while my Black brothers and
sisters had to stay in "their place."

By the time I was old enough to be on my own, the racist lessons I had
learned from my childhood and teen years had become embedded in my mind,

just like all of the teachings of my childhood. When I saw two times two I knew the answer was four; nobody had to teach it to me any longer. When I saw a Black person, I instinctively felt that individual was inferior. The lessons of racism contradicted every moral lesson I had learned. Throughout my life, I had been given many reasons to believe that Black people were less than White people. All of those reasons, every single one of them, turned out to be lies. It was essential to force Black people to stay "in their place," to protect those lies.

As a Chicago lifeguard on Lake Michigan beaches, when Black people came to our all-White beach, we'd chase them off, and some of us would even try to drown them. Why? Because a Black person swimming in those waters would have contradicted the myth that Black people cannot swim and were afraid of water.

White people fought hard to keep Black people out of our schools, because for us to feel special and superior, we had to hold onto the myth that Blacks were unteachable.

We fought hard to keep them out of sports; yet, each time they managed to get into a sport, they excelled. And each time they excelled, whether academically or athletically or in government, politics, or religion, another white lie was proven untrue, and we had to own up to the fact that Black people are human and are created and empowered by God just as we are.

Yet, in spite of all of the evidence contradicting the lies of White supremacy, there are those racists who must hold onto those lies and keep them alive by any means necessary. So, they blind themselves to the truth and try to destroy anything that gets in the way of their lie. They become imprisoned in a state of constant hate when loving your brother and sister feels so much better.

Since the day I began working at Sears, and Mr. Gordon Metcalf forced me to join the Junior Chamber of Commerce, I've watched America come a long way regarding racism, and I know America still has a long, long way to go. I thank God I'm a *recovering* racist and not a *recovered* racist—because that would give me a reason to stop discovering; If I were a recovered racist, I would no longer feel it necessary to meet and talk with people of other races and nationalities; I would stop trying to make a difference. No, I'm not a recovered racist; I'm a *recovering* racist and still have a long way to go to become fully recovered.

Recovering from racism doesn't happen overnight. Even when you begin to face the truth, there will still be times when you want to laugh at racist jokes or deny a Black person a job or loan; or try to keep a Black person from moving into your neighborhood. Just pretend for one minute you are a recovering racist, and deal with the situation like you think a recovering racist would. In other words, fake it until you make it. Pretend you're free of racism and one day, you'll actually be free.

I don't know if somewhere in my subconscious mind I asked God to please help me to recover from my racism. I don't remember ever verbalizing it. But I believe God knew this was what I wanted, and so He didn't put just everyday people into my life to help me with my recovery; He chose the very best advisors for me. He brought into my life, the most outstanding men and women in the world, and most of them happened to be Black. Thank You, God!

I am thankful He placed me in the presence of so many wonderful people who helped me escape from the racist, male chauvinist, anti-Semitic world of prejudice. I chose to enter a brand new, wonderful world where I could march, arm-in-arm with Dr. Martin Luther King, Jr., a man who racists called a troublemaker and a communist.

Instead of laughing at ugly, racist jokes, I laughed at Dick Gregory's humor as he depicted the stupidity of racism.

A Black, Catholic priest named Father George Clements and a Black actor named Lincoln Perry, aka Stepin Fetchit, helped me to become a better Catholic with a stronger faith.

Because of Reverend Jesse L. Jackson, I began to understand what equality of all people really meant.

Muhammad Ali became my friend, as did Chicago's first Black Mayor, Harold Washington.

I learned that Islam is not a religion of hate, because after getting to know and having dined at the dinner table of The Honorable Minister Louis Farrakhan and having become his friend, I discovered he had nothing but love for all people in his heart.

I also learned Stepin Fetchit was not the proper name for a dog, not even my father's big, black Great Dane; because Stepin Fetchit was the stage name of one of the kindest and most talented human beings who walked the face of this earth, none other than, Lincoln Perry, aka "Stepin Fetchit."

If I were still racist, I would have missed out on meeting a wonderful young woman named Hermene Hartman, who became one of my dearest friends and helped get me my own TV show, doing the thing I loved most—talking to people.

If I were still a racist, I would have missed out on hearing a young man speak to a small audience as if he was speaking to thousands, with a message that was so inspiring it prompted me to place one hundred dollars in his hand. If I were a racist, I would have missed out on the joy of seeing that same young man, Barack Obama, become President of the United States of America.

EPILOGUE

"Death leaves a heartache no one can heal,
love leaves a memory no one can steal."
—FROM AN IRISH HEADSTONE

After I retired, I committed to spending as much time as possible with my beautiful wife, Jean. Being with her made me realize how much I loved her and how I became the luckiest man in the world that day I was swimming from the Oak Street Beach and saw this gorgeous blonde named Jean Kloss sitting on the sand at the North Avenue Beach.

She was always in my corner. She was my greatest cheerleader, and she hardly ever complained. Even when she became ill, she valiantly tried to hide her pain behind a caring smile.

My beautiful wife passed away on August 7, 2014. At that time, we belonged to a Catholic church in our community. When I went to make the arrangements, I told the Pastor of that church that I had a very close friend who was a Catholic priest and I wanted him to do the eulogy. "Certainly! That is no problem at all," He told me.

Then I said, "One more thing, Pastor. I have another good friend who is an excellent Black comedian."

He didn't wait for me to finish that part of the request. "No, no! I will not have a Black comedian speak from my church's pulpit!"

I knew there was nothing I could say to change his mind. I also knew the two most important people in my life must have a significant part in the most important event of my life. I was angry and upset. Even though this Pastor had approved Father Clements, he had vehemently denied the participation of Dick Gregory. I shared my frustration with Father Clements, and he just said, "Don't worry, George. I'll take care of it."

Father Clements gave a very moving eulogy. No other priest could have done that because there was not another Catholic priest who knew Jean and our family the way Father Clements did. No one else could have expressed who she was as he did.

When Father Clements finished speaking, he said, "Now, Dick Gregory will give some remarks." To say the Pastor was upset would be an understatement. He was furious! He stormed out of the church and stayed outside during the entirety of Dick Gregory's remarks. After the service, he was so angry he almost made his words incoherent as he said to Father Clements, "I'll call the police on you; you don't belong here." He didn't call the police, but the nerve of this man who could barely speak English telling Father Clements that he didn't belong there.

I knew Gregory could speak well, but still, I was overwhelmed by his remarks. He knew me; he knew Jean, and he talked intimately about the wonderful woman she was. "Everyone gives George credit for all he's done to help others, but Jean is the one who should get all the credit," he said, "She's the one who put up with him being away from home so much. She's the one who allowed him to picket and march for civil rights, to attend meetings, and even to travel halfway across the world."

That August afternoon, he blessed us with his beautiful words of wisdom as only Dick Gregory could. I know Jean O'Hare was looking down from Heaven and listening with that remarkable smile of hers. I could almost hear her saying, "Oh, George, that was really nice!"

~ The End ~

ACKNOWLEDGEMENTS

To everyone who helped me start my journey to recovery from racism and has helped me in one way or another to continue the journey, thank you. Without you, I wouldn't have this story to tell.

Special thanks to Dick Gregory, my best friend in the world who is no longer in this world. Thank you for your friendship, your love, your wisdom, your humor; I miss you tremendously. And thank you for being the inspiration behind this book and for calling John Bellamy to help get this book project going.

To others who helped and supported my journey, and are no longer with us, my dear friend, Ron Orr; my boss and the former Chairman of Sears, Roebuck and Company, Gordon, Metcalf, Father "Dismas" Clark, Fred Hampton, Lincoln Perry, Muhammad Ali, Reverend Willie Taplin Barrow, Daddy O Daylie, Don Cornelius, Herb Kent, Ed Cook, the Reverend Dr. Martin Luther King, Jr, Irv Kupcinet, Mayor Harold Washington, Lu and Jorja Palmer, Edwin C. "Bill" Berry, and so many others. Thank you.

To those who have helped me in one way or another understand the fallacy of racism and the great joy in recovery, Lillian Gregory, Christian Gregory, Reverend Jesse L. Jackson, Sr., Hermene Hartman, Jonathan Jackson, Jacqueline Jackson, Warner Saunders, the Honorable Minister Louis Farrakhan, Sister Claudette Muhammad, Alif Muhammad Joseph Clements, Friday Clements,

Stuart Clements, St. Anthony Clements, Abe Thompson James Compton, Chinta Strausberg, Father Michael Pfleger, Edward Gardner, Sister Lois, Sister Anita Baird, Ruth Love, Renault Robinson, Andrew Barrett, Howard Saffold, Ywain Fields, Cliff Kelly, Mark Wallace, Oprah Winfrey, Purvis Spann, Melody Spann Cooper, Betty Powe, Betty Magness,Art Norman, Perri Small, Salim Muwakkil, Sasha Daltonn, Kirk Townsend, Naurice Roberts, Dorothy Tillman, Cheechee Gwin, Neil Hartigan, Roland Burris, Bill Cosby, Barbara Proctor, Herman Roberts, Josie Childs, Ted Saunders and so many others. Thank you. If I didn't mention your name, charge it to my head but not my heart and I thank you one and all.

Thanks also to Father George Clements, for being my best friend for 60 plus years, and for always being there to support me. Thanks for reading my book before it was a book and contributing your ideas and your words. You know me better than most people; you know my story better than anyone, and nobody was better suited to write the forward to the book than you. Thank you, Father.

I would like to thank John Bellamy for answering Dick Gregory's call and getting the ball rolling as only he could. Thank you for applying your amazing organizational skills and your marketing genius to make *Confessions of a Recovering Racist* a reality. Thank you for introducing me to my wonderful writer, Emma Young.

Thank you Emma Young for listening to my story and putting it into words in a way that even I couldn't put it down and I lived it! Thank you for not only being my writer, but also for becoming my very, very good friend.

Thank you Carole Harrell for the great job you did editing my story.

Thanks to David Hancock, Terry Whalen, Margo Toulouse, Aubrey Kosa, Jim Howard and the entire Morgan James Publishing team. We thank you for seeing some value in my story, and for your patience, your professionalism and guidance in bringing our book to publication.

A very special thanks to my three sons, George III, Bob and Michael. for your love, your support and for doing all that you did to help make your Dad's dream come true.

ABOUT THE AUTHORS

George O'Hare is a retired Sears, Roebuck and Company executive, a motivational speaker, the former Director of Senior Citizen Advocacy for the State of Illinois, former television and radio host for the highly-acclaimed program, *Accentuate the Positive* and recipient of numerous awards and honors, including the May, 1972 "Black Man of the Month" Award. While serving as founder and chairman of the Chicago Junior Chamber of Commerce's Prisoner and Ex-Prisoner Rehabilitation Program, and Volunteer Media Director for Chicago Civil Rights Activists, George began his journey toward recovery from racism. His transition from a White supremacist racist to a Civil Rights advocate and recovering racist, prompted him to tell his story so that others may read it and benefit from his experiences. George is currently a resident of Lisle, Illinois.

Emma Young, is the author of numerous magazine articles, a produced screenplay, *Up Against the Wall,* two memoirs; *Bronx Rhythms and Jim Crow Blues* and *There was No Other Way,* and two children's books, *It's Good to be Me,* and *One Day Kevin Got Mad. Confessions of a Recovering Racist* is her fifth and most important book to date.

Morgan James
Speakers Group

We connect Morgan James published authors with live and online events and audiences who will benefit from their expertise.

CPSIA information can be obtained
at www.ICGtesting.com
Printed in the USA
FSHW012111011219
64654FS